MAKING MANDALAS

27 crochet designs to get your hooks into

US Terms

Emily Littlefair

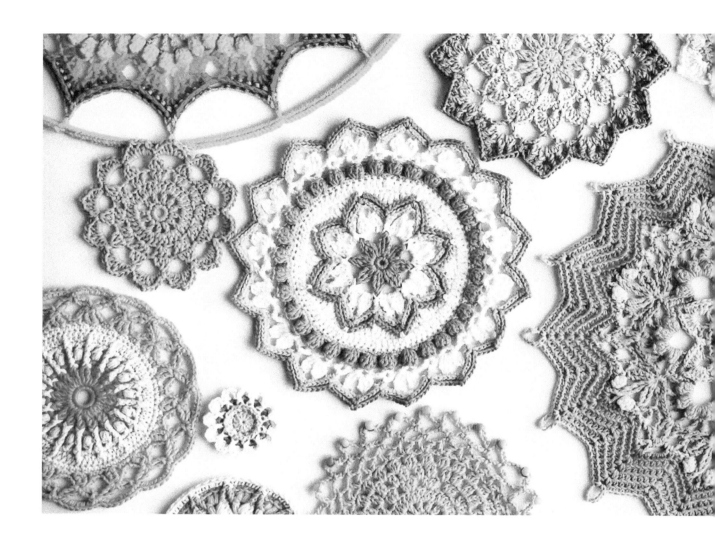

Technical Editing by Emily Reiter

Printed by IngramSpark

First edition 2023

Published by Emily Littlefair
www.theloopystitch.com

Paperback ISBN: 978-0-6457877-0-2
Hardcover ISBN: 978-0-6457877-4-0

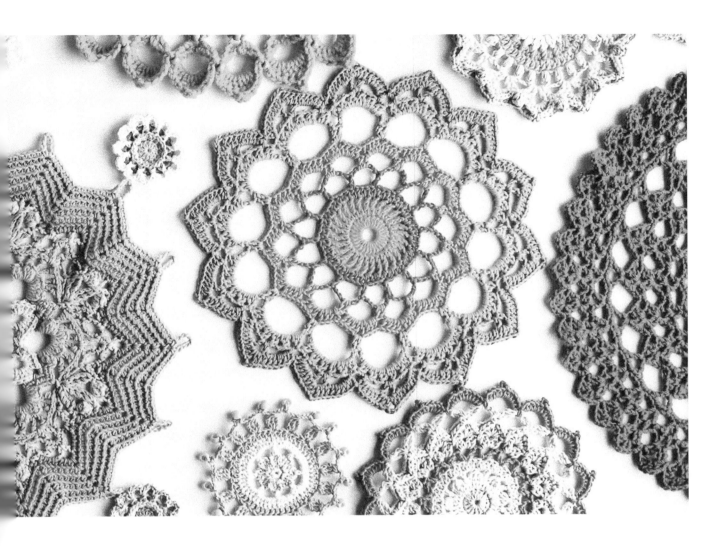

DEDICATION

This book is dedicated to my boys, everything I do is for you.
You will never know how much I love you.
Thank you for being the best gift I have ever received.

In the spirit of reconciliation, I respectfully acknowledge the Traditional Custodians of
country throughout Australia and their connections to land, sea and community.
I pay my respects to their Elders past and present and extend that respect to all
Aboriginal and Torres Strait Islander people.

ACKNOWLEDGEMENTS

This endeavour would not have been possible without the love and support from Richard, my husband. For letting me get lost in hours of designing, yarn and mandalas EVERY-WHERE, impromptu photoshoots, and for all the hours it has taken to put it all together into an actual book and all the time it took for me to learn how to do it all myself. For his understanding when sometimes it felt like I bit off more than I could chew. For being there through all the highs and lows and for taking me as the crazy crochet lady that I am. I look foward to spending weekends with you and the boys again. Hopefully you haven't forgotten who I am haha.

Words cannot express my gratitude to my amazing team of testers. This has been a feat I could not have achieved without you. You are my rocks, my many sets of extra keen eyes, vigilant hooks and hands and even though we all live around the world, we're forever connected by our special bond. In no particular order, I praise Margaret Richards, Audrey Muller, Mirjam Annaars, Lyn Merton, Natasha Ireland, Krystle Patrono, Narelle Mitchell, Kathy Mant, Antoinette Loggenberg, Melissa Pearce, Melissa Coles, Silke Spit, Natalie Rowland, Jane Reid, Amanda, Renée Roy, Ruth Bracey, Susan Marcille, Kim Siebenhausen, Tracey Whiting and Paulina Smith Maraboli.

I could not have undertaken this journey without Shelley Husband and her guidance and help throughout this entire process. Thank you for your reassurance when I suffered self-doubt, was at the low-points, and couldn't see the end in sight. Even though this has been

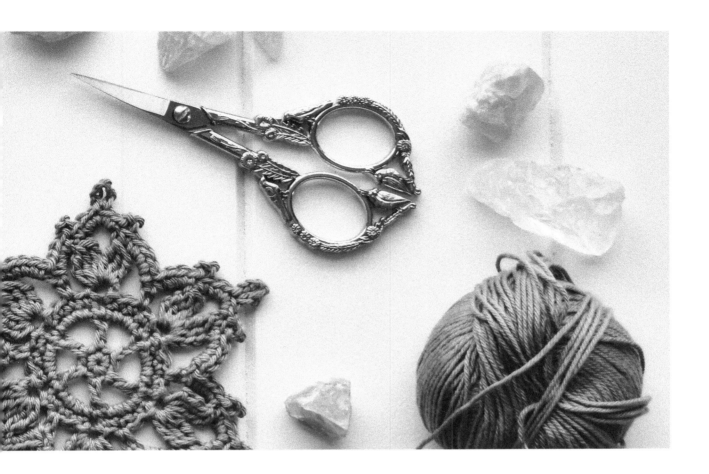

such a learning curve, this would not have been possible without you. I would have thrown the towel in a long time ago.

I am also so grateful for my dear friend Joy Clements. Like Shelley, you were there to hear me whinge, share in the excitement when I had something new to share, such as another update with my process throughout the entire self-publishing journey and be there to pick me up and assure me that I was on the right path and to listen to my heart. I love that crochet has brought you into my life.

I would like to extend my sincere thanks to the rest of my family, for your continued support and encouragement. I hope to do you proud each and every day and also by constantly showing you what I am capable of because of what you have instilled within me.

Special thanks goes to Emily Reiter, my amazing tech-editor. For your sharp eyes and drive to be the best that you can be. I am looking forward to working with you in the future on many books and other patterns to come. I promise that next time, I will not give you all the patterns at once unless you are up for another challenge.

Last, but certainly not least, I would like to express my deepest appreciation to all of you who have supported me over the years by purchasing my patterns, sharing your makes (that makes my heart sing), commented on my social media posts and those who have shared in the memorable moments of completing workshops and retreats with me. Your continued support inspires me to continue designing and to be the best that I can be. Much love,

Em xxx

CONTENTS

MANDALAS

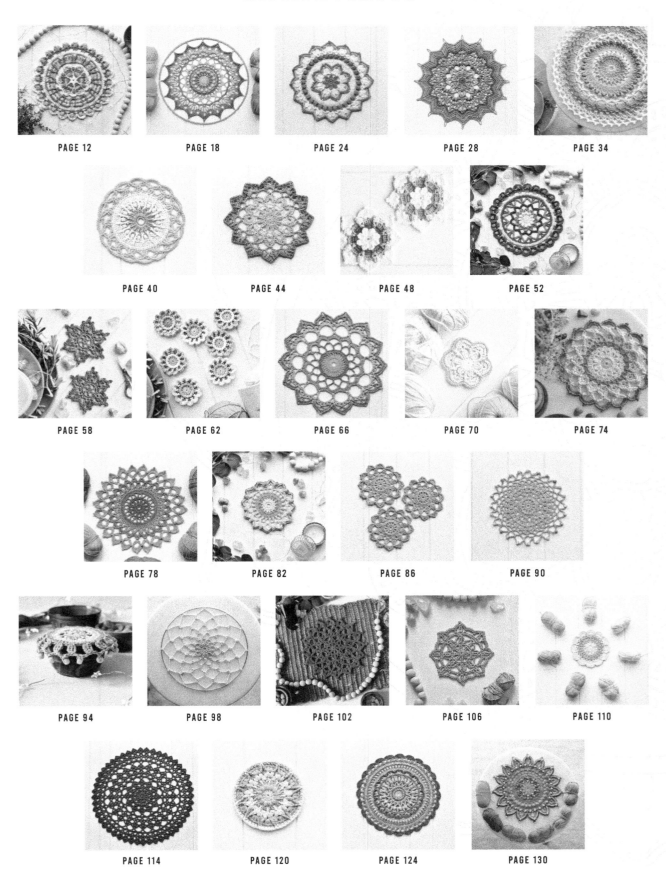

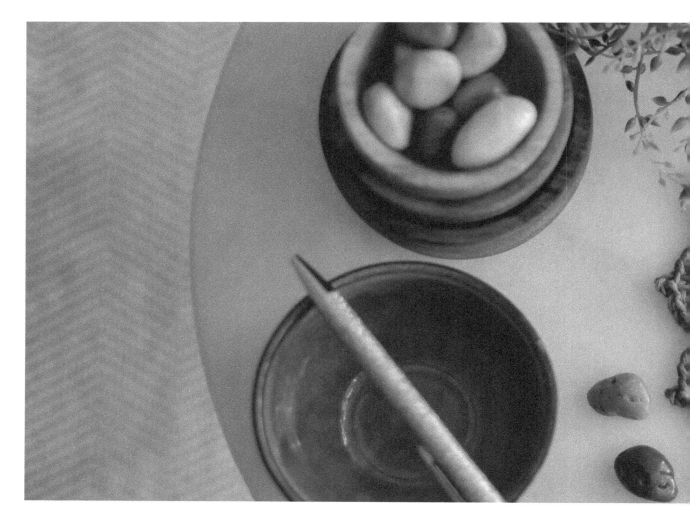

WELCOME

h e l l o

Oh my gosh! I did it! There were multiple times during the entire process where I thought of throwing in the towel, but it was at those moments, pushing through the darkness, when the light shone brightest.

KEEP IN THE LOOP

Follow me on Social Media and Website for all things Loopy Stitch.

Instagram	Facebook	Website

It does not matter how slowly you go as long as you do not stop.

~ CONFUCIUS ~

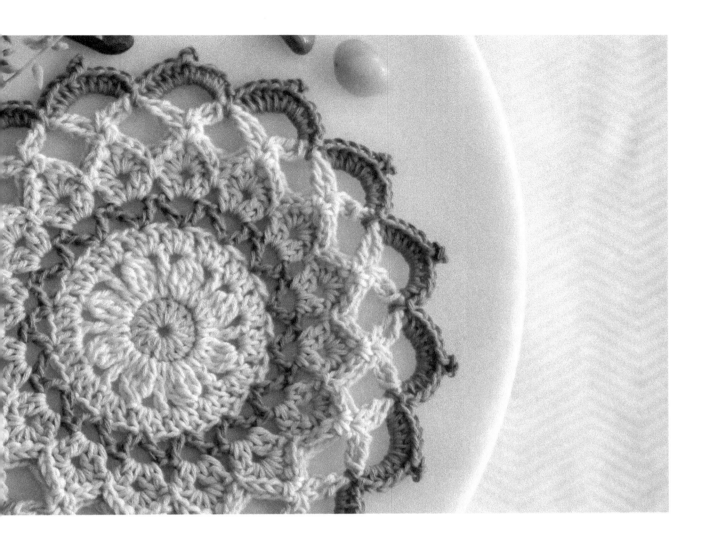

DESIGN NAMES

I chose to name my designs after virtues and morals, something that means a lot to me and how I live my life and would like to instil in my boys as they grow older.

I have also included their definitions which were sourced from dictionary.com.

Not only that but I tried my best to relate them to crochet for a little laugh and also a quote or saying as well. Little personal touches that I hope may spark that light inside you that you might have been looking for.

BEST WISHES

I really hope you enjoy making all the pieces in the book, some are small and do not take much time and others require a little more concentration.

Be mindful of your crochet time, enjoy it, soak it up, and be present in every moment.

I wish the crochet fairies find you at night to weave in your ends and find the missing hooks that the lounge takes without you even noticing. But most importantly...

...Happy Hooking! Much love,

Em xxx

COLOUR

It's no secret I love colour. It speaks to me.

It's the first thing I choose before I begin designing and I really believe the following quote.

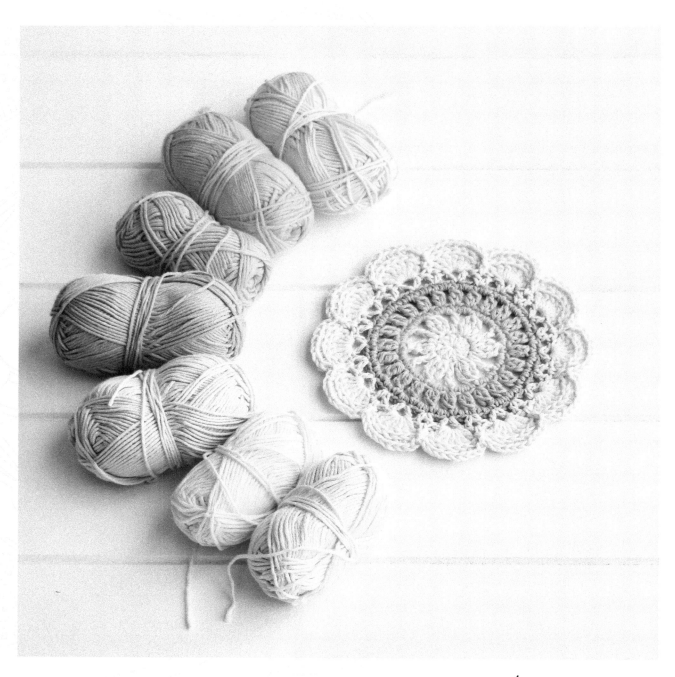

Colour possesses a language without words.

BILLY DUGGER

ABOUT ME

Designer, Author, Photographer, Graphic Designer (all self-taught lol)

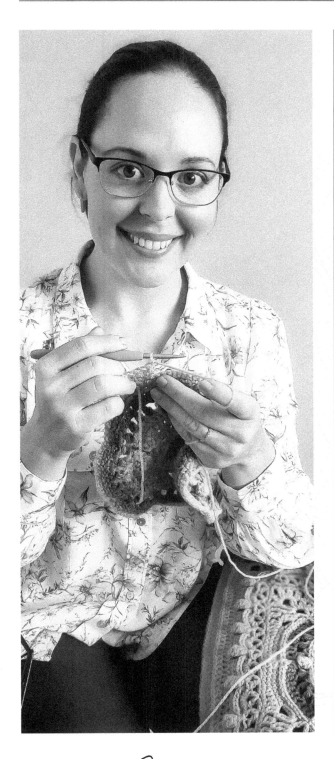

Emily

Hi there. My name is Emily and I love designing crochet patterns, especially mandala designs. I find something calming and mindful about working in rounds. They bring me so much joy.

This is my first self-published book and because I love learning and doing everything myself, it has definitely been a learning curve. Not knowing what to expect or how to do it, I do love a good challenge.

I have a favourite saying 'without challenge, we cannot grow' and boy have I grown whilst doing this book. But seriously, there were some days I just loved it, some where I would rather have forgotten about it altogether, but persistence of wanting to see these designs on your hooks were inspiration and motivation to keep going.

I am a mum to three active, beautiful, football-crazy boys who light up my life more than they will ever know. I need to keep my hands busy, to help with my overactive mind, so designs pour off my hooks and sometimes I cannot keep up and forget to write them down. Hindering my future self when I go to write them up for testing and publishing. I love nature and am grateful for all the beauty that surrounds me.

I am happily married to another football-crazy person. So during football (round ball/soccer) season and pre-season, our lives are crazy busy, but it seems our family thrives on it. So we just keep on doing it. Milo (dog) and Molly (cat) are also part of our lives and I can't imagine life without them.

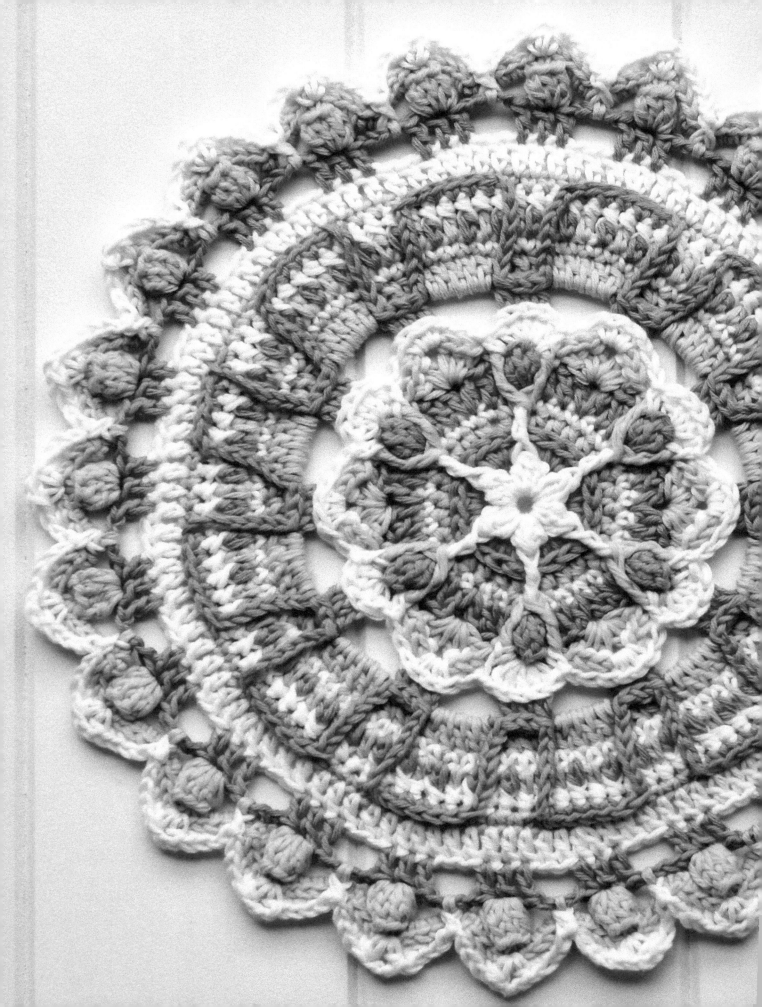

ABUNDANCE

MANDALA

noun. an extremely plentiful or oversufficient quantity or supply

An abundance of yarn.

FINISHED SIZE

30cm/11.8in unblocked

MATERIALS

Naturals Organic Cotton
One ball of each

Colour 1 7168 Gypsum

Colour 2 7199 Deep Sea

Colour 3 7175 Citron

US G-6 / UK 8 / (4mm) hook

Yarn Needle

Scissors

Stitch Marker

NOTES & TIPS

Third Loop

Work in the loop behind the 'V' as stated.

Round 14

Do not make the chain stitches too tight or too loose in this round. If they are made too tight, they could cause the mandala to start cupping.

Back Loop Only

When making stitches into the back loop only, work into the third loop as well to secure it nicely.

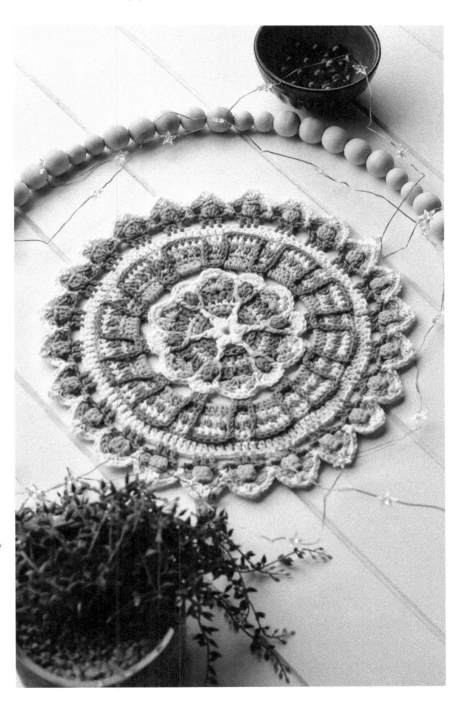

You can never have too much yarn.

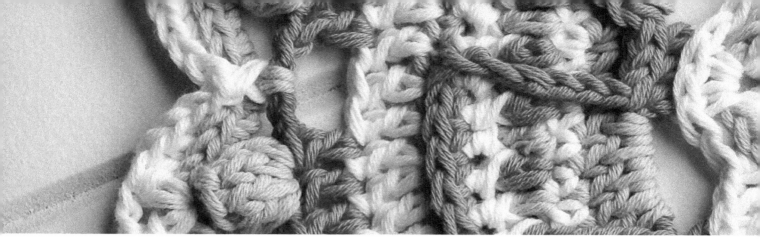

Round 1: C1

Make a MR, or (ch 5, join to first ch to form ring), beg dc3cl in ring, ch 3, (dc3cl, ch 3) five times in ring, join to first cl to form ring, fasten off. *<6 dc3cl, 6 ch-3 sp>*

Round 2: C2

In any cl, make a standing [fphdc around cl, 3 hdc in ch-3 sp] around, join to first fphdc made, fasten off. *<6 fphdc, 18 hdc>*

Round 3: C3

Blo hdc in any fphdc, blo hdc in same st, blo hdc in next 3 sts, [2 blo hdc in next st, blo hdc in next 3 sts] around, join to first blo hdc made, fasten off. *<30 blo hdc>*

Round 4: C1 - *No st is skipped from Rnd 3 when fptr are made*

Sc in first st from prev round, fptr around cl from Rnd 1, [sc in next 5 sts, fptr around cl] around, on final repeat, sc in last 4 un-worked sts, join to first sc made, fasten off. *<6 fptr, 30 sc>*

Round 5: C2

In any fptr, make a standing [pop in fptr, dc in next 2 sts, (dc, ch 1, dc) in next st, dc in next 2 sts] around, join to first pop made, fasten off. *<6 pop, 36 dc, 6 ch-1 sp>*

Round 6: C3

In any ch-1 sp, make a standing [(3 dc, ch 2, 3 dc) in ch-1 sp, sk 2 sts, sc in next st, fptr around fptr from Rnd 4, sc in pop, fptr around same fptr, sc in next st, sk 2 sts] around, join to first dc made, fasten off.

<36 dc, 6 ch-2 sp, 18 sc, 12 fptr>

Round 7: C1

In fptr before pop, make a standing [fpsc around fptr before pop, 5 dc in sc, fpsc around next fptr, sk 2 sts, bphdc around next 2 sts, 3 hdc in ch-2 sp (place marker in first hdc made only), bphdc around next 2 sts, sk 2 sts] around, join to first fpsc made, fasten off. *<12 fpsc, 30 dc, 24 bphdc, 18 hdc>*

Round 8: C2– *This round is worked in the 3rd loop*

In marked st, make a standing hdc (place marker in st), hdc in next 2 sts, ch 4, sk 4 sts, [hdc in next 3 sts, ch 4, sk 4 sts] around, join to first hdc made, fasten off. *<36 hdc 3rd loop, 12 ch-4 sp>*

Round 9: C3

In marked st, make a standing dc in 3rd loop of st (place marker in st), dc in 3rd loop of next 2 sts, 5 dc in ch-4 sp, [dc in 3rd loop of next 3 sts, 5 dc in ch-4 sp] around, join to first dc made in 3rd loop, fasten off. *<60 dc, 36 blo dc>*

Round 10: C1

In first st from prev rnd, make a standing sc, [2 sc in next st, sc in next 7] around, on final repeat, omit last sc, join to first sc made, fasten off. *<108 sc>*

Round 11: C2

In first st from prev rnd, make a standing [dc, ch 1, sk st] around, join to first dc made, fasten off. *<54 dc, 54 ch-1 sp>*

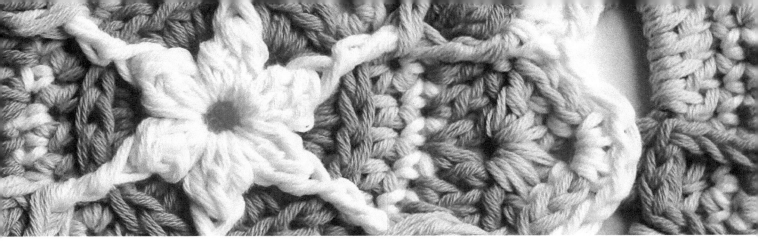

Round 12: C3 - *Fold Rnd 11 to the back, this Rnd is worked into the unworked sts from Rnd 10.*

In first unworked st, make a standing [dc, ch 1 (place marker in first ch-1 sp only), sk st] around, join to first dc made, fasten off. *<54 dc, 54 ch-1 sp>*

Round 13: C1

Fphdc around any dc from Rnd 11 or 12, fphdc around each st from Rnds 11 & 12 around, join to first fphdc made, fasten off. *<108 fphdc>*

Round 14: C2 – *This Rnd is worked into Rnds 8 & 13, also note there are 4 unworked sts between sets of 5 sc*

Join with sl st to any first hdc from Rnd 8, sl st in next 3 sts (the 4th st will be the first ch st in Rnd 8 after last hdc), ch 7 (not too loose or tight), working into Rnd 13, sc directly into st aligned with last sl st just made, sc in next 4 sts in Rnd 13, ch 7 (not too loose or tight), [sl st to first hdc of group from Rnd 8, sl st in next 3 sts, ch 7, sc in aligned Rnd 13 st from last sl st, sc in next 4 sts in Rnd 13, ch 7] around, join to first sl st, fasten off. *<48 sl st, 24 ch-7 sp, 60 sc>*

Round 15: C3 – *This Rnd is worked into Rnds 12, 13 and 14.*

In marked ch-sp from Rnd 12, make a standing [hdc in first ch-1, (hdc in next st, hdc in ch-1 sp) two times, pick up 3rd loop (bump) from first ch st of ch-7 made in prev rnd,

make sc into unworked fphdc in Rnd 13, sc in next 2 sts, pick up 3rd loop (bump) of last ch st of ch-7 made in prev rnd and sc in next fphdc] around, join to first hdc made, fasten off. *<48 sc, 60 hdc>*

Round 16: C1

In last sc before hdc in prev rnd, make a standing dc, dc in next 2 sts, [2 dc in next st, dc in next 8] around, on final repeat omit last 3 dc, join to first dc made, fasten off. *<120 dc>*

Round 17: C2

In first dc of 2 dc from prev rnd, make a standing dc, dc in next 2 sts, ch 3, sk 2 sts, [dc in next 3 sts, ch 3, sk 2 sts] around, join to first dc made, fasten off. *<72 dc, 24 ch-3 sp>*

Round 18: C3

In any middle dc, make a standing [pop in middle dc, ch 3, sc in ch-3 sp, ch 3] around, join to first pop, do not fasten off. *<24 pop, 48 ch-3 sp, 24 sc>*

Round 19: C3

Ch 1 (doesn't count as st), [(sc, ch 2, sc) in pop, 3 sc in ch-3 sp, fpsc around sc, 3 sc in ch-3 sp] around, join to first sc made, fasten off. *<192 sc, 24 ch-2 sp, 24 fpsc>*

Round 20: C1

[(hdc, ch 2, hdc) in ch-2 sp, blo hdc in next 2 sts, blo sc in next st, ch 1, sk st, fpsc around fpsc, ch 1, sk st, blo sc in next st, blo hdc in next 2 sts] around, join to first hdc made, fasten off. *<48 hdc, 96 blo hdc, 48 blo sc, 24 fpsc, 48 ch-1 sp, 24 ch-1 sp>*

ABUNDANCE
MANDALA

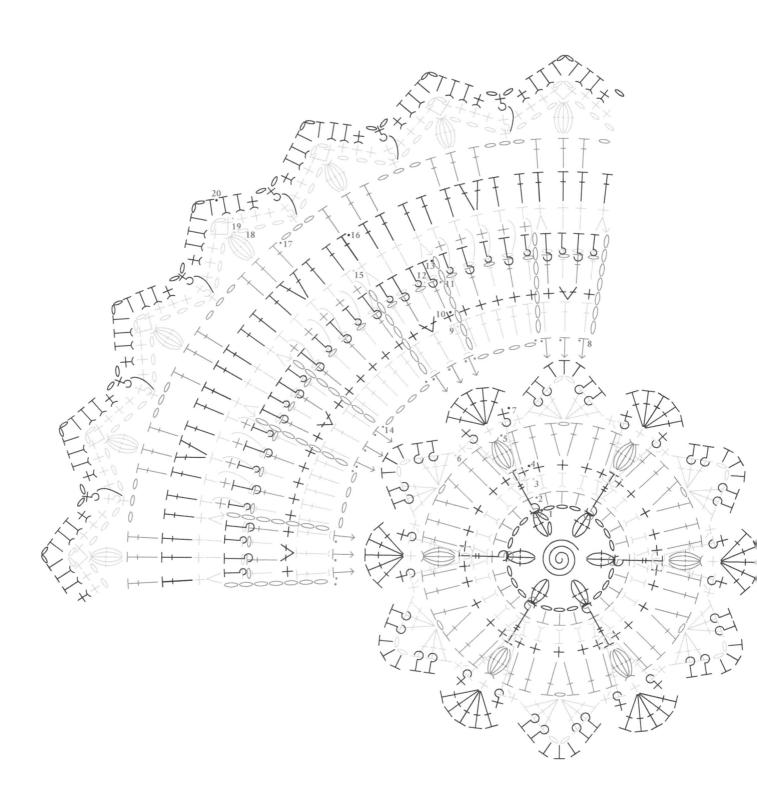

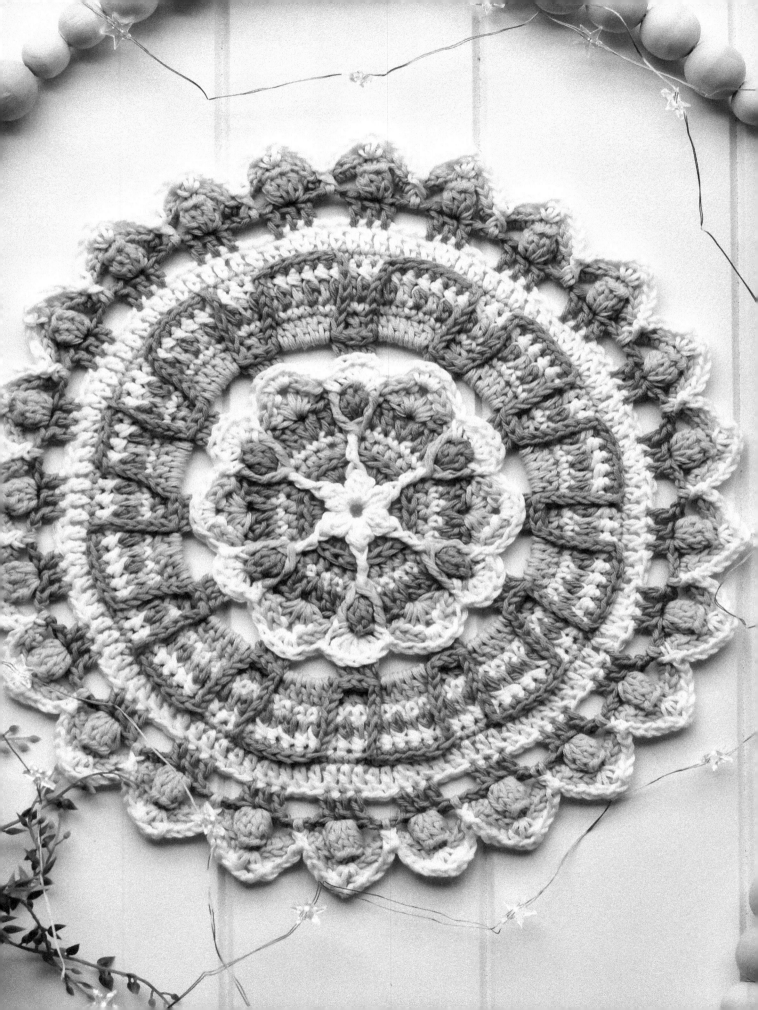

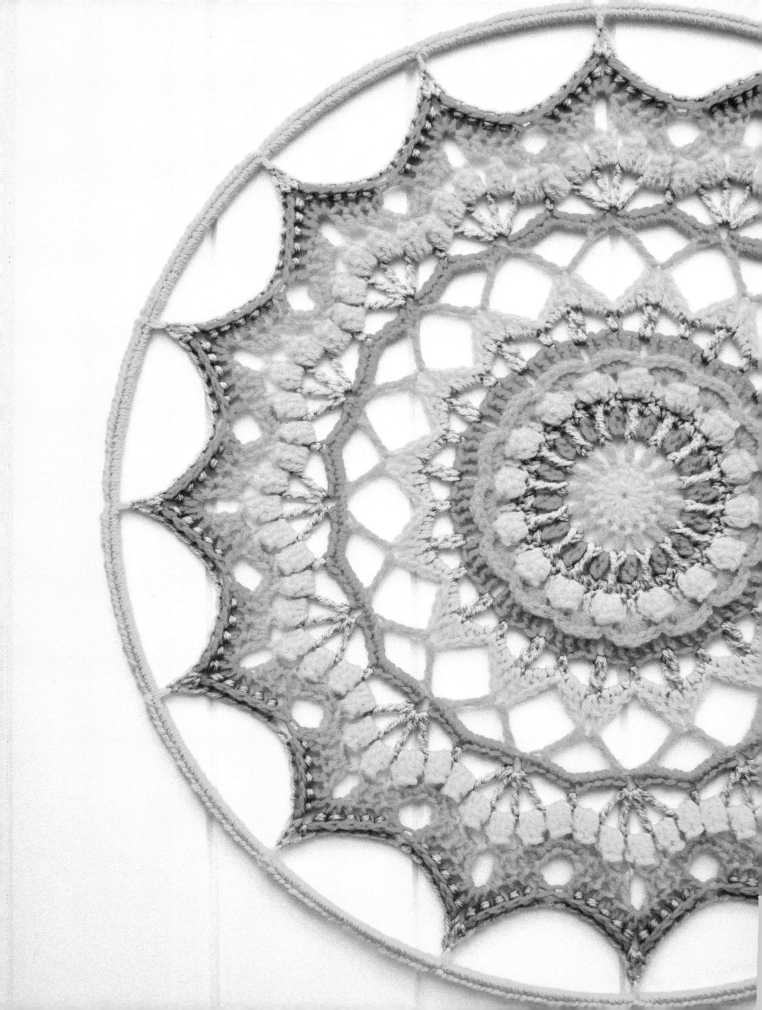

APPRECIATION
MANDALA

noun. gratitude; thankful recognition

The more I crochet, the more I have appreciation for what this magic wand and long stuff can turn into.

FINISHED SIZE

42cm/16.5in unblocked

MATERIALS

Special DK
One ball of each

Colour 1 1856 Dandelion
Colour 2 1711 Spice
Colour 3 1723 Tomato
Colour 4 1725 Sage

US 7 / UK 7 / (4.5mm) hook
Yarn Needle
Scissors
Stitch Marker/s
Ring is optional 50cm/19.7in used

NOTES & TIPS

Standing Stitches
If you are using different colours for each round, try to use standing stitches instead of starting chains.

Invisible Joins
These go hand in hand with Standing Stitches and hide the joins on each round.

Attaching to ring
Use stitch markers to attach your finished piece to the ring to see if it will fit nicely.

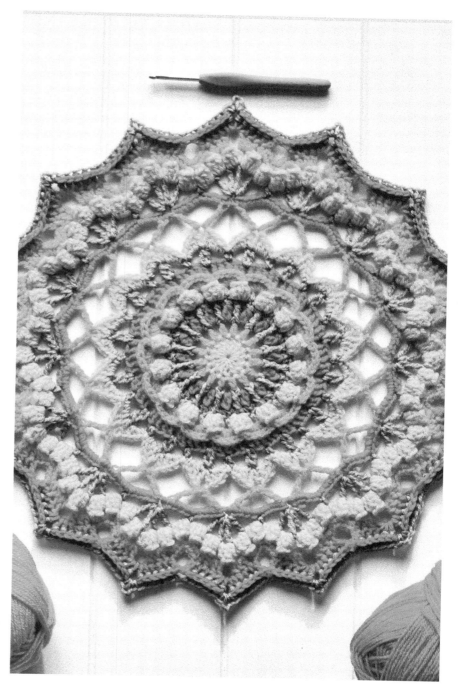

Trade your expectations for appreciation and your whole life will change.

Tony Robbins

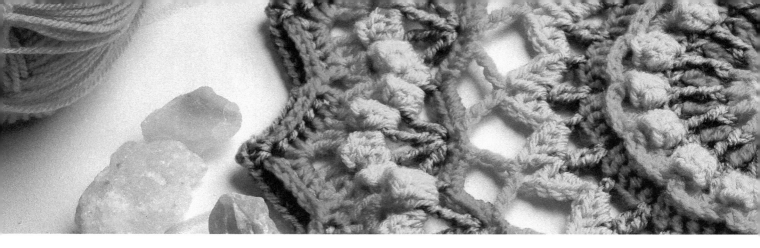

Round 1: C1

Make a MR, or (ch 5, join to first ch to form ring), ch 3 (counts as dc), 15 dc in ring, join to top of ch 3, fasten off. *<16 dc>*

Round 2: C2

In any st, make a standing (dc + ch 1) in each st around, join to first dc made, fasten off. *<16 dc, 16 ch-1 sp>*

Round 3: C3

In any ch-1 sp, make a standing (dc2cl + ch 2) in each ch-1 sp around, join to first dc2cl made, fasten off. *<16 dc2cl, 16 ch-2 sp>*

Round 4: C4

In any cl, make a standing [fpsc around cl, sc in next ch-2 sp, fptr around dc from Rnd 2, sc in same ch-2 sp] around, join to first fpsc made, fasten off. *<16 fpsc, 16 fptr, 32 sc>*

Round 5: C1

In any fptr, make a standing [pop in fptr, ch 2, sk st, sc in fpsc, ch 2, sk st] around, join to first pop made, fasten off. *<16 pop, 16 sc, 32 ch-2 sp>*

Round 6: C – *This rnd may be slightly ruffled*

In any sc, make a standing [5 dc in sc, sk ch-2 sp, sc in pop, sk ch-2 sp] around, join to first dc made, fasten off. *<80 dc, 16 sc>*

Round 7: C3

Make a standing bpdc around first dc of any 5-dc group, bpdc around next 4 sts, sk sc, [bpdc around next 5 dc, sk sc] around, join to

first bpdc, fasten off. *<80 bpdc>*

Round 8: C4 – *Cl sts are made between sts, not in sts*

Make a standing [dc2cl in between first and last dc, ch 3, sk 2 sts, sc in next st (3rd dc), ch 3, sk 2 sts] around, join to first dc2cl made, fasten off. *<16 dc2cl, 16 sc, 32 ch-3 sp>*

Round 9: C1

Join with a [sl st to sc, (sc, hdc, dc) in ch-3 sp, (dc, ch 2, dc) in cl, (dc, hdc, sc) in ch-3 sp] around, join to first sc with sl st and fasten off. *<16 sl st, 32 sc, 32 hdc, 64 dc, 16 ch-2 sp>*

Round 10: C2

In any ch-2 sp, make a standing [(tr, ch 6, tr) in ch-2 sp, ch 1] around, join to first tr made, fasten off. *<32 tr, 16 ch-6 sp, 16 ch-1 sp>*

Round 11: C3

In any ch-1 sp, make a standing [sc in ch-1 sp, sc in st, 7 sc in ch-6 sp, sc in st] around, join to first sc made, fasten off. *<160 sc>*

Round 12: C4

In first sc made prev rnd, make a standing [(tr, ch 1) 4 times in sc, sk 4 sts, sc in next st, ch 1, sk 4 sts] around, join to first tr made, fasten off. *<64 tr, 16 sc, 80 ch-1 sp>*

Round 13: C1

After any sc, make a standing [(pop in ch-1 sp, ch 3, sk st) 4 times, pop in next ch-1 sp, ch 2] around, join to first pop made, fasten off. *<80 pop, 64 ch-3 sp, 16 ch-2 sp>*

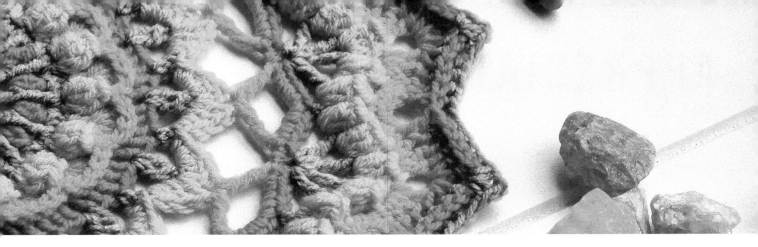

Round 14: C2

Make a standing [sc in ch-2 sp, sk pop, (2 sc, hdc) in ch-3 sp, sk pop, (hdc, 2 dc) in ch-3 sp, ch 2, sk pop, (2 dc, hdc) in ch-3 sp, sk pop, (hdc, 2 sc) in ch-3 sp, sk pop] around, join to first sc made, fasten off. *<80 sc, 64 hdc, 64 dc, 16 ch-2 sp>*

Round 15: C3

In first hdc made in prev rnd, make a standing dc, dc in next 3 sts, (2 dc, ch 2, 2 dc) in ch-2 sp, dc in next 4 sts, sk 5 sts [dc in next 4 sts, (2 dc, ch 2, 2 dc) in ch-2 sp, dc in next 4 sts, sk 5 sts] around, join to first dc made, fasten off. *<192 dc, 16 ch-2 sp>*

Round 16: C4

In any ch-2 sp, make a standing [(sc, ch 2, sc) in ch-2 sp, bphdc around next 5 sts, ch 1, sk 2 sts, bphdc around next 5 sts] around, join to first sc made, fasten off. *<160 bphdc, 32 sc, 16 ch-2 sp>*

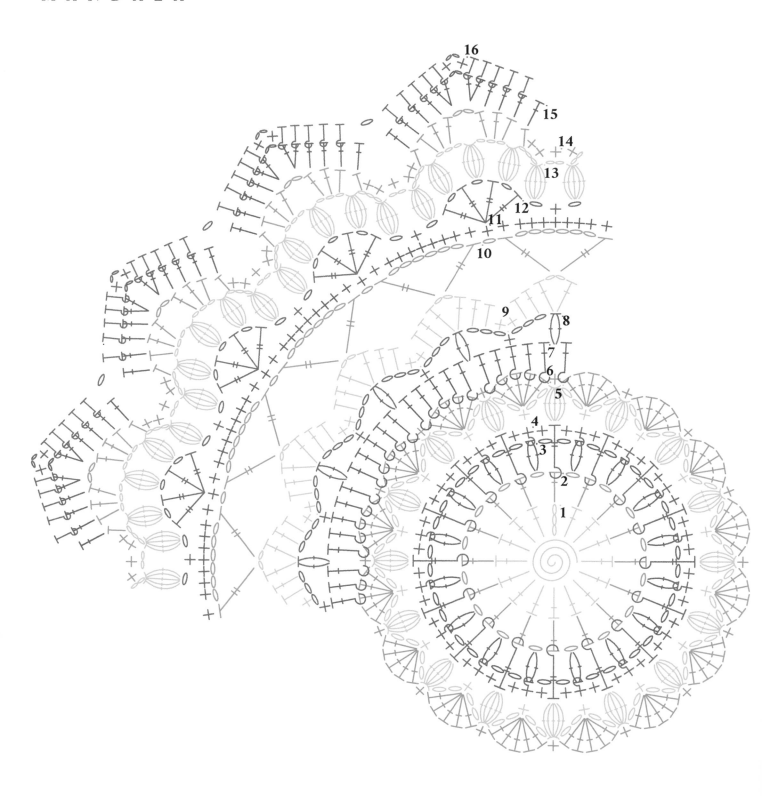

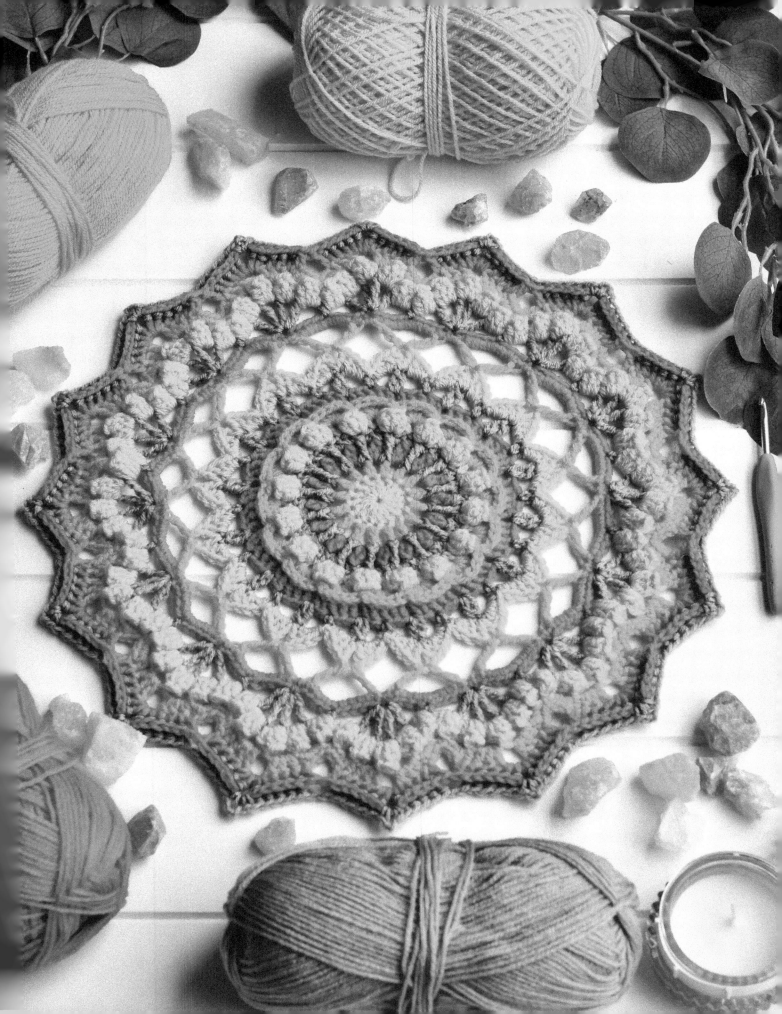

AWARENESS
MANDALA

noun. the state or condition of being aware; having knowledge; consciousness

Awareness of what crochet is capable of is truly amazing and inspiring

FINISHED SIZE

26.5cm/10.4in unblocked

MATERIALS

Naturals Organic Cotton
One ball of each

Colour 1 7199 Deep Sea
Colour 2 7168 Gypsum
Colour 3 7175 Citron

US G-6 / UK 8 / (4mm) hook
Yarn Needle
Scissors
Stitch Marker

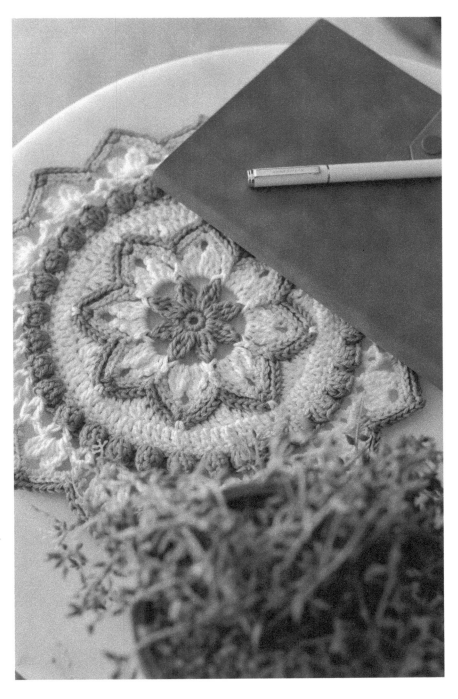

NOTES & TIPS

Third Loop
Work in the loop behind the 'V' as stated.

Standing Stitches
If you are using different colours for each round, try to use standing stitches instead of starting chains.

Invisible Joins
These go hand in hand with Standing Stitches and hide the joins on each round.

Awareness is the greatest agent for change.

Eckhart Tolle

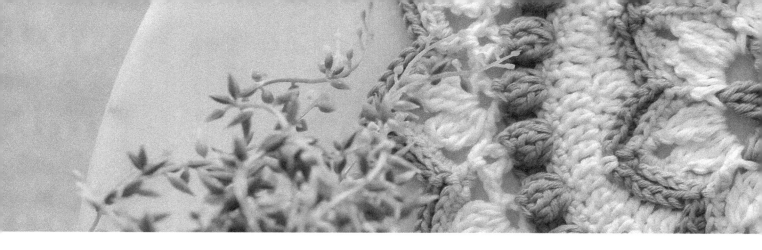

Round 1: C1

Make a MR, or (ch 4, join to first ch to form ring), ch 1, (doesn't count as st), 8 sc in ring, join to first sc made, do not fasten off. *<8 sc>*

Round 2: C1

Beg tr3cl in same st as join, ch 3, (tr3cl, ch 3) in each st around, join to first cl made, fasten off. *<8 tr3cl, 8 ch-3 sp>*

Round 3: C2 – *Feel free to replace the standing tr3cl with a beg tr3cl if you prefer* [(tr3cl, ch 3, tr3cl) in ch-3 sp, ch 3, fpdc around cl from Rnd 2, ch 3] around, join to first cl made, fasten off. *<16 tr3cl, 24 ch-3 sp, 8 fpdc>*

Round 4: C3

Make a standing [(2 sc, ch 2, 2 sc) in ch-3 point, sc in st, 2 sc in ch-3 sp, fpsc around fpdc, 2 sc in ch-3 sp, sc in st] around, join to first sc made, fasten off. *<80 sc, 8 fpsc, 8 ch-2 sp>*

Round 5: C1

Make a standing [(hdc, ch 2, hdc), in ch-2 point, hdc in 3rd loop next 5 sts, sl st in fpsc, hdc in 3rd loop next 5 sts] around, join to first hdc made, fasten off. *<80 hdc 3rd loop, 16 hdc, 8 sl st, 8 ch-2 sp>*

Round 6: C2 – *This round is worked in the 3rd loop except in the ch-2 point*

Make a standing [sc in ch-2 point, sc in next st, hdc in next 2 sts, dc in next st, tr2tog over next 5 sts skipping the 3 in middle, dc in next st, hdc in next 2 sts, sc in next st] around, join to first sc made, fasten off. *<16 3rd loop sc, 32 3rd loop hdc, 16 3rd loop dc, 8 3rd loop tr2tog, 8 sc>*

Round 7: C2 – *Still using this colour and to hide the obvious join*

[Dc in sc, dc in next 4 sts, 2 dc in next st, dc in next 4 sts] around, join to first dc made, fasten off. *<88 dc>*

Round 8: C3

Make a standing sc in first dc from prev rnd, sc in next 5 sts, 2 sc in next st, [sc in next 10 sts, 2 sc in next st] around, on final repeat sc 4, join to first sc made, fasten off. *<96 sc>*

Round 9: C1

In second sc in Rnd 8 [pop in sc, ch 1, dc in 3rd loop next 2 sts] around, join to first pop made, fasten off. *<32 pop, 32 ch-1 sp, 64 dc>*

Round 10: C2 – *Start in a pop that aligns with the Rnd 5 point*

Make a standing (dc, ch 2, dc, ch 1) in each pop around, join to first dc made, fasten off. *<64 dc, 32 ch-2 sp, 32 ch-1 sp>*

Round 11: C2 – *This round is worked only in ch-2 sps*

Sl st to ch-2 sp, make a (beg tr3cl, ch 3, tr3cl) in same ch-2 sp, ch 3, sc in next ch-2 sp, ch 3, [(tr3cl, ch 3, tr3cl) in next ch-2 sp, ch 3, sc in next ch-2 sp, ch 3] around, join to first cl made, fasten off. *<32 tr3cl, 16 sc, 48 ch-3 sp>*

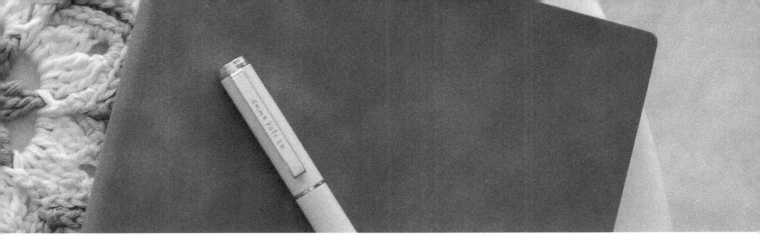

Round 12: C3

Make a standing [fpsc around sc from prev Rnd, 3 sc in ch-3 sp, sc in st, (2 sc, ch 2, 2 sc) in ch-3 sp, sc in st, 3 sc in ch-3 sp] around, join to first fpsc made, fasten off. *<192 sc, 16 ch-2 sp, 16 fpsc>*

Round 13: C1

Make a standing [(sc, ch 2, sc) in ch-2 sp, sc 3rd loop in next 5 sts, sk st, sl st in fpsc, sk st, sc 3rd loop in next 5 sts] around, join to first sc made, fasten off. *<160 3rd loop sc, 32 sc, 16 ch-2 sp, 16 sl st>*

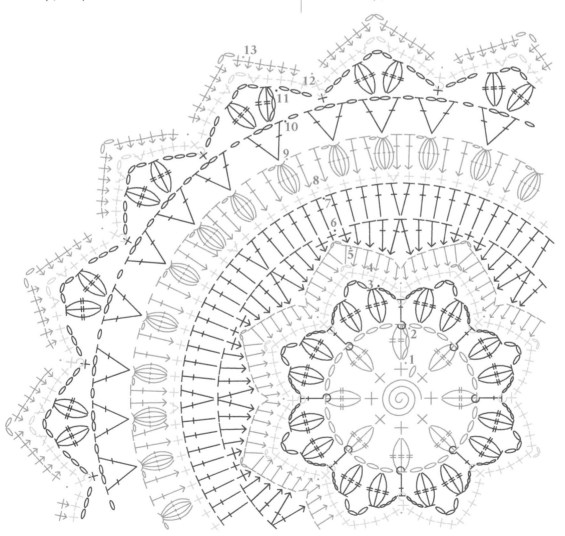

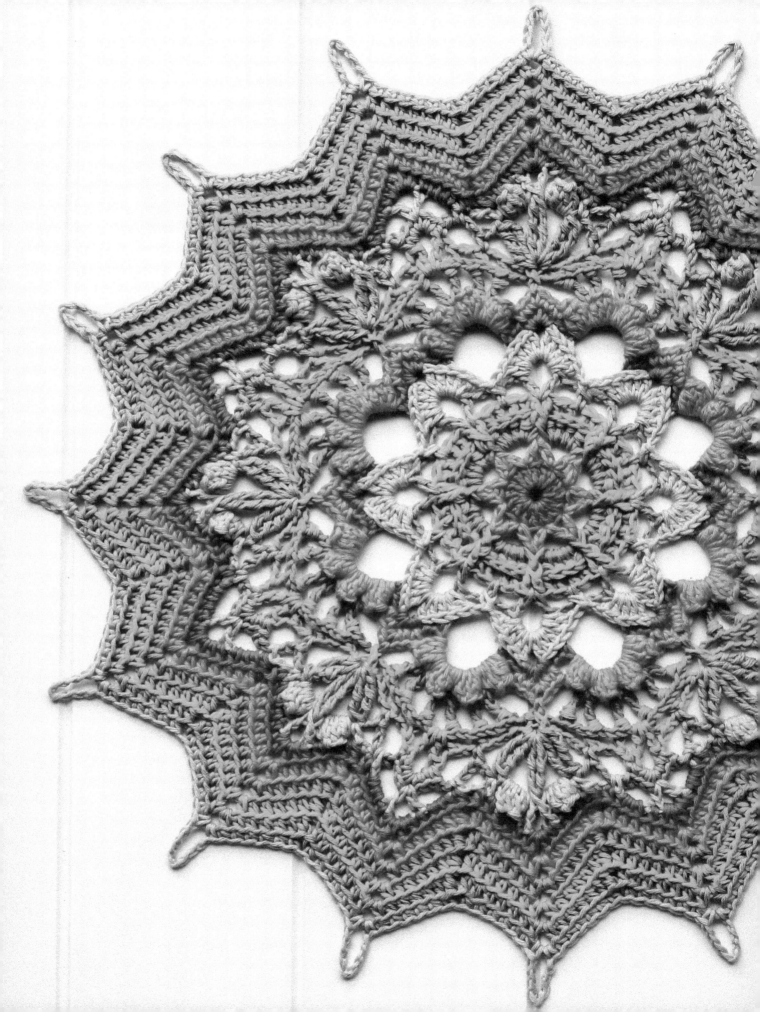

BALANCE

MANDALA

noun. a state of equilibrium or equipoise; equal distribution of weight, amount, etc.

Sometimes it's a hard job trying to find a balance between our wips, ufos and new projects.

FINISHED SIZE

42cm/16.5in unblocked

MATERIALS

Organic Cotton
One ball of each

Colour 1 7201 Indigo Wash

Colour 2 7198 Azure

Colour 3 7192 Sea Green

Colour 4 7191 Jade

Colour 5 7171 Leaf

Colour 6 7175 Citron

US G-6 / UK 8 / (4mm) hook

Yarn Needle

Scissors

Stitch Marker

NOTES & TIPS

Third Loop

Work in the loop behind the 'V' as stated.

Back Loop

When crocheting into the back loop, also pick up the third loop to keep it more secure.

Blocking

Feel free to give the chain loops a nice block after finishing.

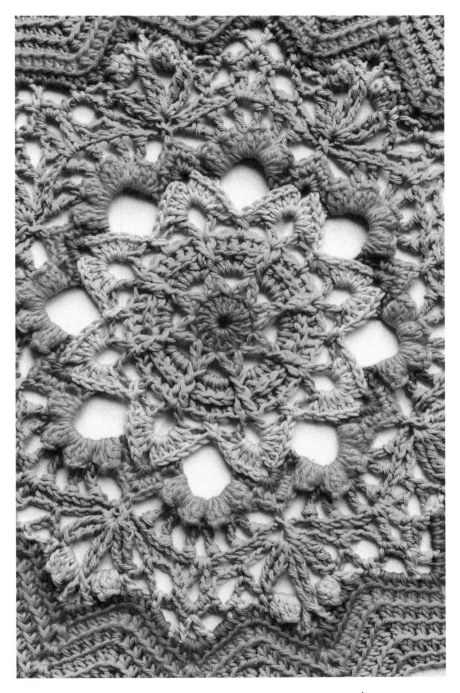

Balance is not something you find, it's something you create.

Jana Kingsford

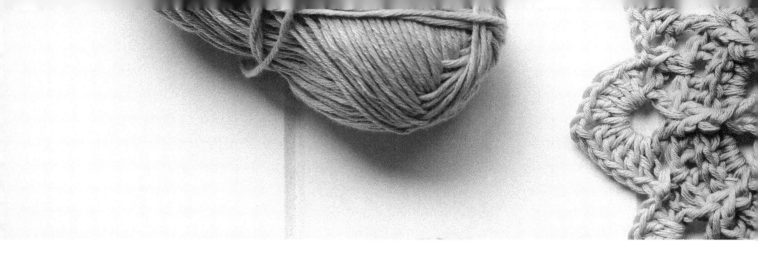

Round 1: C1

Make a MR, or (ch 5, join to first ch to form ring), ch 3 (counts as st), 15 dc in ring, join to top of ch 3, fasten off. *<16 dc>*

Round 2: C2

In any st, make a standing [(dc, ch 3, dc) in st, sk st] around, join to first dc made, fasten off. *<16 dc, 8 ch-3 sp>*

Round 3: C3

In ch-3 sp, make a standing [4 dc in ch-3 sp, fpdc around next 2 sts as one] around, join to first dc made, fasten off. *<8 fpdc, 32 dc>*

Round 4: C4

Around any fpdc, make a standing [2 fpdc around fpdc, bpdc around next 4 sts] around, join to first fpdc made, fasten off. *<16 fpdc, 32 bphdc>*

Round 5: C5

In between two fpdc, make a standing [(dc, ch 4, dc) in between two fpdc, ch 2, sk 3 sts, sc in between second and third bpdc, ch 2, sk 3 sts] around, join to first dc made, fasten off. *<16 dc, 8 sc, 16 ch-2 sp, 8 ch-4 sp>*

Round 6: C6

Around any sc, make a standing [fpsc around sc, ch 1, sk ch-sp and st, (5 dc, ch 2, 5 dc) in ch-4 sp, ch 1, sk st and ch-sp] around, join to first fpsc made, fasten off. *<80 dc, 16 ch-2 sp, 8 fpsc>*

Round 7: C1 – *Place markers in ch-1 sps*

In any ch-2 point, make a standing [(2 sc, ch 1, 2 sc) in ch-2 point, sc in third loop next 3 sts, ch 7, sk 7 sts, sc in third loop of third dc and next 2 sts] around, join to first sc made, fasten off. *<32 sc, 48 third loop sc, 8 ch-1 sp, 8 ch-7 sp>*

Round 8: C2 – *Place markers in ch-1 sps*

In any ch-1 point, make a standing [(sc, ch 1, sc) in ch-1 point, sc in next 2 sts, ch 2, sk 3 sts, (pop, ch 2) four times in ch-7 sp, sk 3 sts, sc in next 2 sts] around, join to first sc made, fasten off. *<32 pop, 48 sc, 40 ch-2 sp, 8 ch-1 sp>*

Round 9: C3

In any ch-1 point, make a standing [sc in ch-1 point, ch 2, sk 3 sts, sk ch-sp, sk pop, (tr, ch 2, tr, ch 2) in each of the next 3 ch-2 sps, sk pop, sk ch-sp, sk 3 sts] around, join to first sc made, fasten off. *<48 tr, 56 ch-2 sp, 8 sc>*

Round 10: C4

Around any sc, make a standing [fpsc around sc, (ch 2, sk ch-sp, bpdc around st) three times, ch 1, (tr, ch 3, tr) in ch-2 sp, ch 1, (bpdc around next st, ch 2, sk ch-sp) three times] around, join to first fpsc made, fasten off. *<48 bpdc, 16 tr, 48 ch-2 sp, 16 ch-1 sp, 8 fpsc, 8 ch-3 sp>*

Round 11: C5

In any fpsc, make a standing [(dtr2cl, ch 3, dtr2cl, ch 3, dtr2cl) in fpsc, ch 2, sk ch-sp, sk st, sk ch-sp, sc in bpdc, ch 5, sk ch-sp, sk st, sk ch-sp, sc in tr, (2 sc, ch 1, 2 sc) in ch-3 sp,

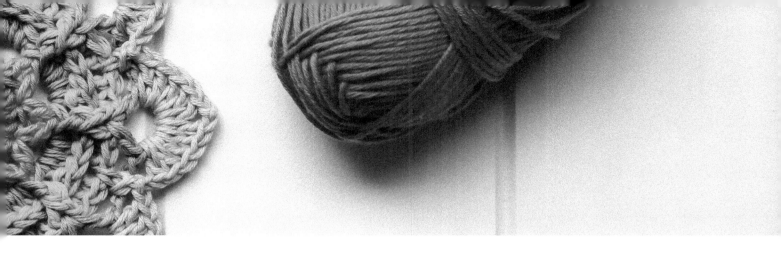

sc in tr, ch 5, sk ch-sp, sk st, sk ch-sp, sc in bpdc, ch 2, sk ch-sp, sk st, sk ch-sp] around, join to first dtr2cl made, fasten off. *<24 dtr-2cl, 64 sc, 16 ch-2 sp, 16 ch-5 sp, 16 ch-3sp>*

Round 12: C6

In any ch-1 point, make a standing [(dc, ch 3, dc) in ch-1 point, ch 3, sk 3 sts, sc in ch-5 sp, ch 2, sk st and ch-sp, sc in cl, ch 1, pop in ch-3 sp, ch 2, (fpdc, ch 2, fpdc) around cl, ch 2, pop in ch-3 sp, ch 1, sc in cl, ch 2, sk ch-sp and st, sc in ch-5 sp, ch 3, sk 3 sts] around, join to first dc made, fasten off. *<16 dc, 32 sc, 16 pop, 16 ch-1 sp, 32 ch-2 sp, 8 ch-2 point, 8 ch-3 point, 16 ch-3 sp, 16 fpdc>*

Round 13: C1

In any ch-3 point, make a standing [(2 hdc, ch 2, 2 hdc) in ch-3 point, hdc in st, 3 hdc in ch-3 sp, hdc in next st, sk ch-sp, hdc in next st, hdc in ch-sp, hdc in pop, hdc in ch-sp, hdc in st, (2 hdc, ch 2, 2 hdc) in ch-2 point, hdc in st, hdc in ch-sp, hdc in pop, hdc in ch-sp, hdc in st, sk ch-sp, hdc in next st, 3 hdc in ch-3 sp, hdc in next st] around, join to first hdc made, fasten off. *<224 hdc>*

Rounds 14-17:

In any ch-2 point, make a standing [(hdc, ch 2, hdc) in ch-2 point, blo hdc in next 6 sts, sk 2 sts, blo hdc in next 6 sts] around, join to first hdc made, fasten off. *<196 blo hdc, 32 hdc>*

Rnd 14 - C2

Rnd 15 - C3

Rnd 16 - C4

Rnd 17 - C5

Round 18: C6

In any ch-2 sp, make a standing [(sc, ch 8, sc) in ch-2 sp, blo sc in next 6 sts, sk 2 sts, blo sc in next 6 sts] around, join to first sc made, fasten off. *<192 blo sc, 32 sc, 16 ch-8 sp>*

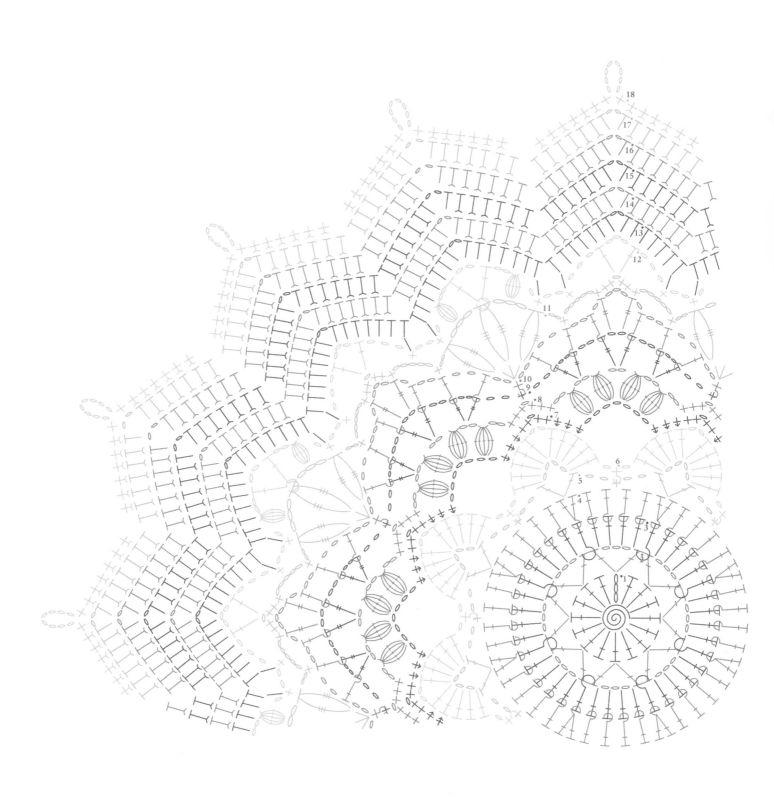

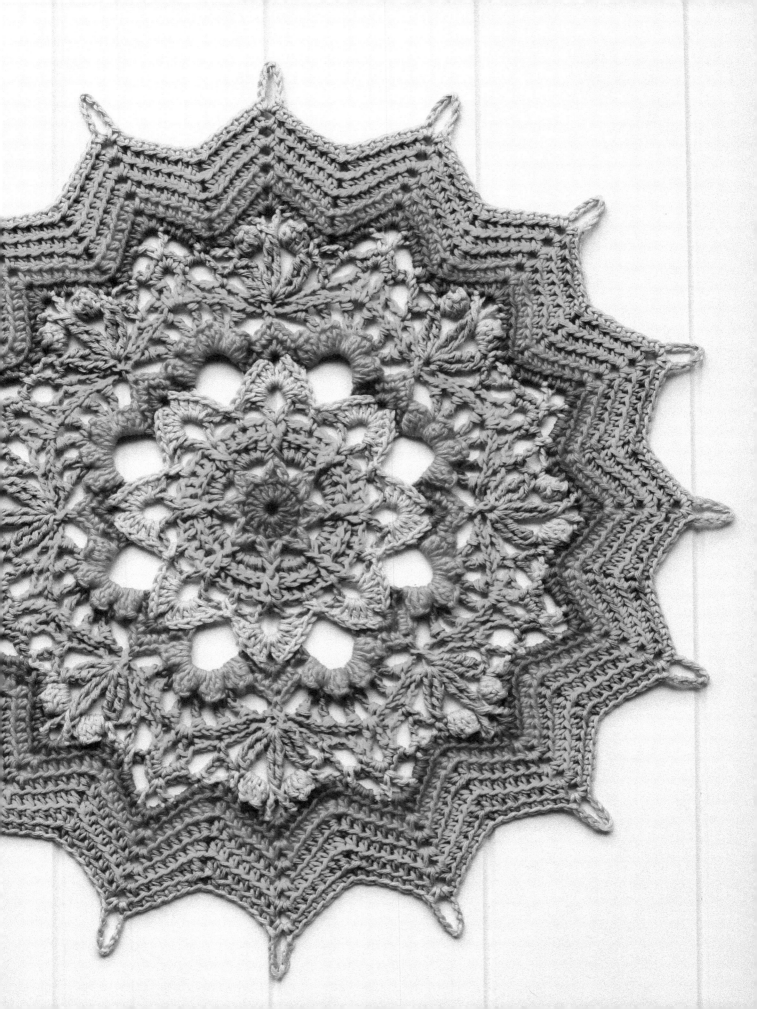

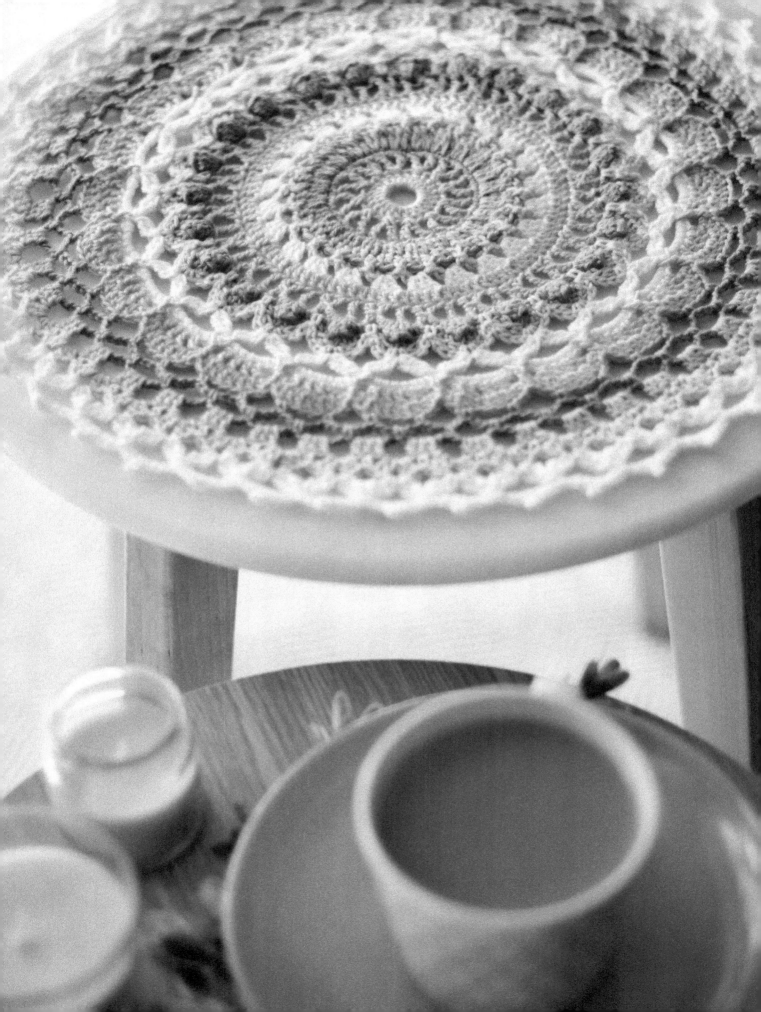

COMFORT

MANDALA

verb. to soothe, console, or reassure; bring cheer to

crochet and comfort; you can't have one without the other, unless you're using black yarn

FINISHED SIZE

42cm/16.5in unblocked

MATERIALS

Naturals Bamboo & Cotton
One ball of each

Colour 1 7131 Peach
Colour 2 7133 Blush
Colour 3 7138 Heather
Colour 4 7139 Wedgewood
Colour 5 7141 Aqua
Colour 6 7127 Chalk

US E-4 / UK 9 / (3.5mm) hook
Yarn Needle
Scissors
Stitch Marker

NOTES & TIPS

Magic Ring
Pull Magic Ring after Round 2 nice
and tight, but not too tight, enough
to keep all the stitches nice and
uniform.

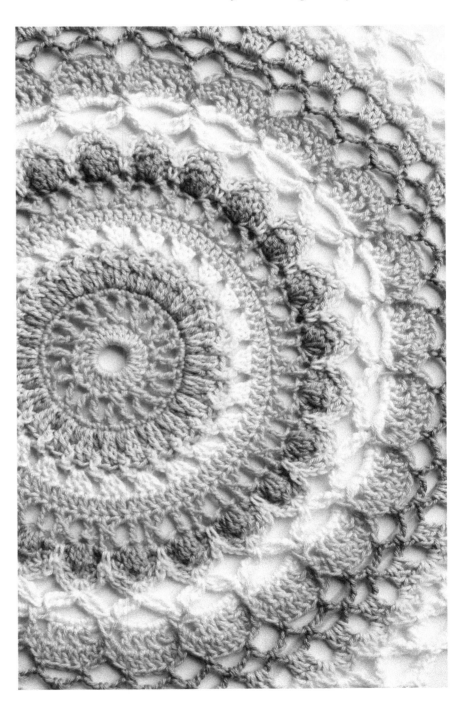

Cure sometimes, treat often, comfort always.

Hippocrates

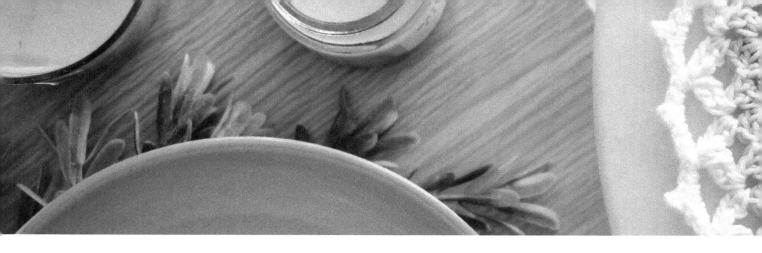

Round 1: C1 - *Leave a longer tail than normal so you can pull the ring tighter after Rnd 3.*

Make a MR, or (ch 10, join to first ch to form ring), ch 3 *(counts as dc)*, 23 dc in ring, join to top of ch 3, fasten off. *<24 dc>*

Round 2: C2

In any st, make a standing cross over tr, cross over tr around, join to first tr made, do not fasten off. *<12 cross over tr>*

Round 3: C2

Ch 1 *(doesn't count as st)*, sc in same st as join, 2 sc in ch-1 sp, [sc in next 2 sts, 2 sc in ch-sp] around, on final repeat sc in last st, join to first sc made, fasten off. *<48 sc>*

Round 4: C3

In first sc made, make a standing [puff 3, ch 2, sk st] around, join to first puff 3 made, fasten off. *<24 puff 3, 24 ch-2 sp>*

Round 5: C4

Around any puff, make a standing [fphdc around puff, fold ch-2 sts back, 2 tr in unworked st from Rnd 4] around, join to first fphdc made, fasten off. *<48 tr, 24 fphdc>*

Round 6: C5

Around any fphdc, make a standing [fpsc around fphdc, ch 1, (dc, ch 1, dc) in unworked ch-2 sp from Rnd 4, ch 1] around, join to first fpsc, fasten off. *<24 fpsc, 72 ch-1 sp, 48 dc>*

Round 7: C6 – *This rnd is worked only in ch-1 sps between two dc sts from Rnd 6.*

Make a standing [3 dc in ch-1 sp between two dc sts, ch 1] around, join to first dc made, fasten off. *<72 dc>*

Round 8: C1

In any ch-1 sp, make a standing [dc in ch-1 sp, dc in next 3 sts] around, join to first dc made, fasten off. *<96 dc>*

Round 9: C2 – *This rnd may cup up slightly.*

In first dc made in prev rnd, make a standing [tr in dc made in ch-sp, x st over next 3 sts] around, join to first tr made, fasten off. *<24 tr, 24 x st>*

Round 10: C3

In any tr, make a standing [pop in tr st, ch 2, sc in next st, ch 2, sk ch-2 sp, sc in next st, ch 2] around, join to first pop made, fasten off. *<24 pop, 72 ch-2 sp, 48 sc>*

Round 11: C4 – *This rnd may be slightly ruffled*

In any pop, make a standing [(dc, ch 2, dc) in pop, dc in ch-2 sp, sk st, (hdc, sc, hdc) in ch-2 sp, sk st, dc in ch-2 sp] around, join to first dc made, fasten off. *<24 sc, 48 hdc, 96 dc, 24 ch-2 sp>*

Round 12: C5 – *This rnd may still be slightly ruffled*

In any ch-2 sp, make a standing [(sc, ch 2, sc) in ch-2 sp, sc in 3rd loop of next 2 sts, ch 2, sk hdc, sc in ch-2 sp from Rnd 9, ch 2, sk sc and hdc, sc in 3rd loop of next 2 sts] around, join to first sc made, fasten off. *<72 sc, 96*

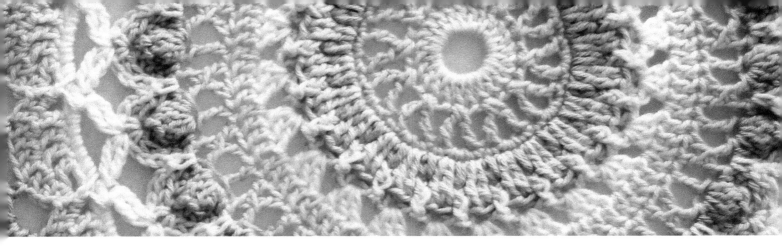

3rd loop sc, 72 ch-2 sp>

Round 13: C6

In any ch-2 point, make a standing [(tr2cl, ch 6, tr2cl) in ch-2 point] around, join to first tr2cl made, do not fasten off. *<48 tr2cl, 24 ch-6 sp>*

Round 14: C6

Ch 1 (doesn't count as st), sc in same st as join, 6 sc in ch-6 sp, [sc in next 2 sts, 6 sc in ch-6 sp] around, on final repeat sc in last st, fasten off. *<192 sc>*

Round 15: C1 – *Fpdc st made around last cl in ch-2 point, and next cl in next ch-2 point together.*

Around first and last cl made, make a standing [fpdc around both clusters together, ch 1, sk 2 sts, (dc, ch 1) in each of next 4 sts, sk 2 sts] around, join to first fpdc made, fasten off. *<24 fpdc, 96 dc, 120 ch-1 sp>*

Round 16: C2

Around any fpdc, make a standing [fpsc around fpdc, hdc in ch-1 sp, {dc in next st, dc in next ch-sp} three times, dc in next st, hdc in ch-1 sp] around, join to first fpsc made, fasten off. *<24 fpsc, 48 hdc, 168 dc>*

Round 17: C3

In 3rd st after fpsc, make a standing [sc in st, ch 5, sk 3 sts, sc in next st, ch 5, sk 5 sts] around, on final repeat ch 2, dc in first sc made, do not fasten off. *<48 sc, 48 ch-5 sp>*

Round 18: C3

Sc over dc just made *(this will bring you to middle of last ch-5 sp from prev rnd)*, ch 5, [sc in ch-5 sp, ch 5] around, join to first sc made, fasten off. *<48 sc, 48 ch-5 sp>*

Round 19: C4

In any ch-5 sp, make a standing [(3 dc, ch 3) in each ch-5 sp] around, join to first dc made, fasten off. *<144 dc, 48 ch-3 sp>*

Round 20: C5

In any ch-3 sp, make a standing [(2 dc, ch 2, 2 dc) in ch-3 sp, sk st, sc in middle st, sk st] around, join to first dc made, fasten off. *<192 dc, 48 ch-2 sp, 48 sc>*

Round 21: C6

In any ch-2 point, make a standing [(tr2cl, ch 5, tr2cl) in ch-2 point] around, join to first tr2cl made, do not fasten off. *<96 tr2cl, 48 ch-5 sp>*

Round 22: C6

Around first and last cl made, make a standing [fpsc around both clusters together from prev rnd, (3 sc, picot 3, 3 sc) in ch-5 sp] around, join to first fpsc made, fasten off.

<48 picot 3, 288 sc, 48 fpsc>

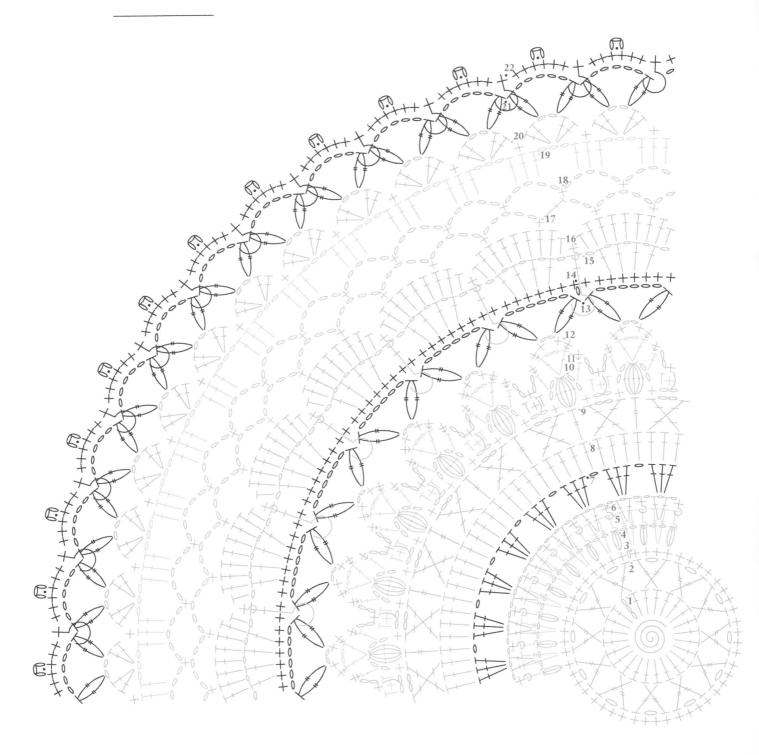

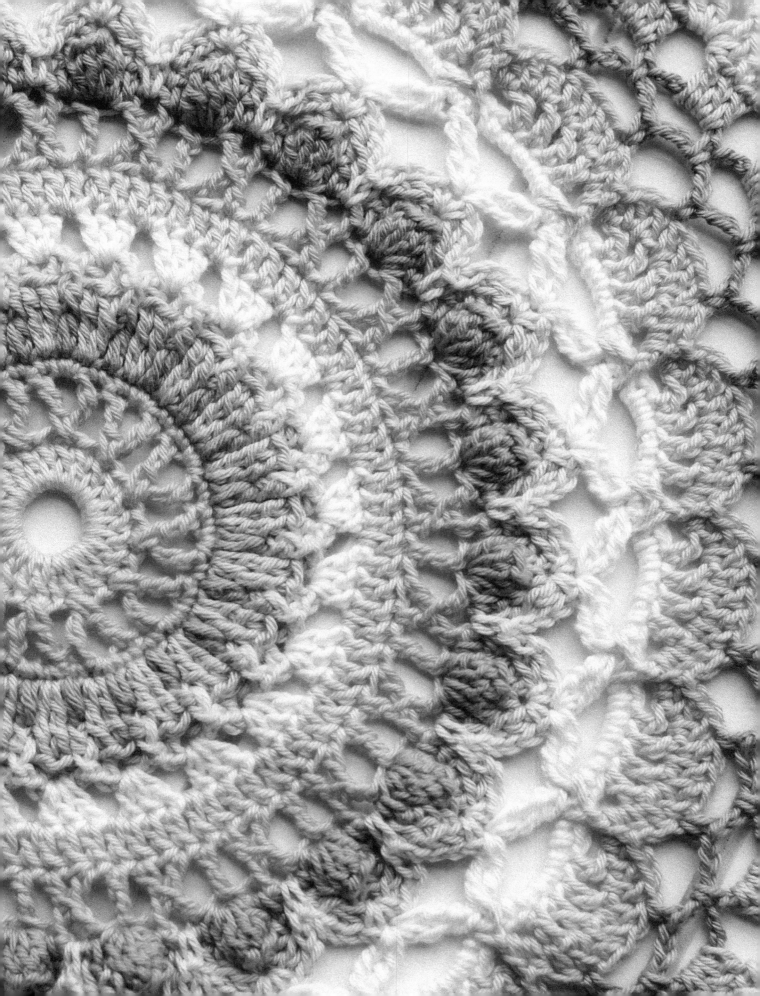

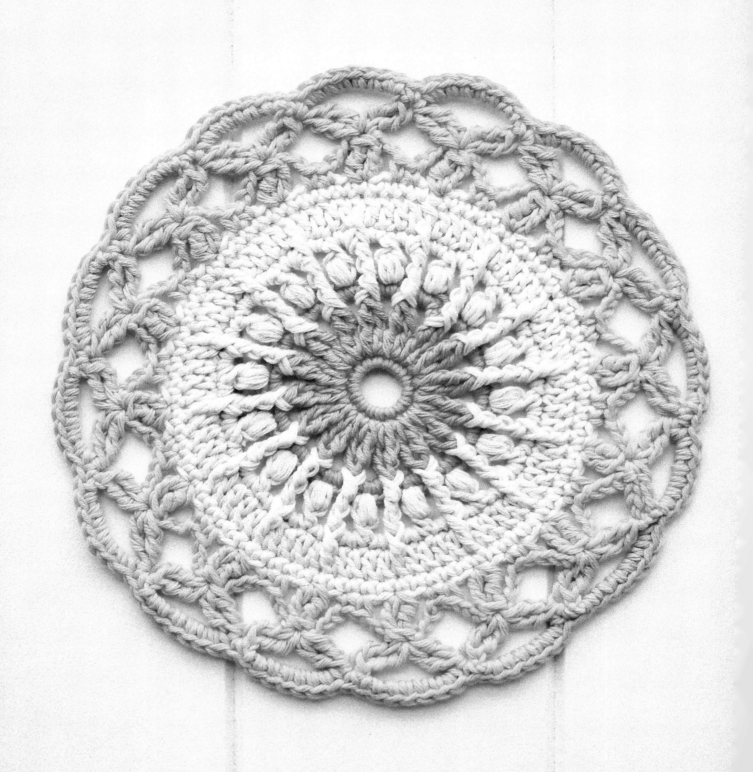

DEDICATION

MANDALA

noun. the state of being dedicated

Something you see when a crocheter is counting the same round or row of stitches for the 20th time, shhh!

FINISHED SIZE

21cm/8.2in unblocked

MATERIALS

Naturals Organic Cotton
One ball of each

Colour 1 7198 Azure

Colour 2 7195 Faded Denim

Colour 3 7183 Blossom

Colour 4 7169 Fondant

US G-6 / UK 8 / (4mm) hook

Yarn Needle

Scissors

Stitch Marker

NOTES & TIPS

Cluster Stitches

Is your top loop too big and loose? Try holding all the yarn over loops on your hook with a finger before inserting your hook into the stitch. As you make the yarn over and pull through loop, push remaining loops towards the end of the hook, still securing the remaining loops on the hook with your finger.

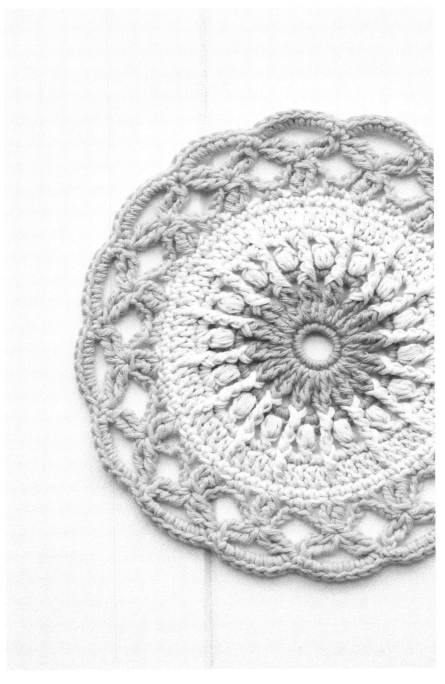

Dedication, absolute dedication, is what keeps one ahead.

Bruce Lee

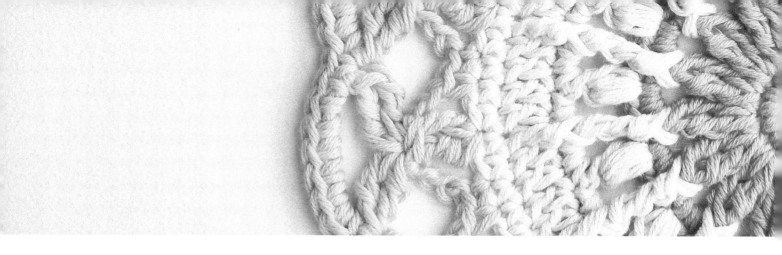

Round 1: C1

Make a MR, or (ch 12, join to first ch to form ring), ch 1 (doesn't count as st), 16 sc in ring, join to first sc made, do not fasten off.

<16 sc>

Round 2: C1

Beg tr2cl in same st as join, ch 2, (tr2cl in next st, ch 2) around, join to beg tr2cl, do not fasten off. *<16 tr2cl, 16 ch-2 sp>*

Round 3: C1

Ch 1 (doesn't count as st), 3 sc in each ch-2 sp around, join to first sc made, fasten off.

<48 sc>

Round 4: C2

Around any cl from Rnd 2, make a standing [fpdtr around cl from Rnd 2, ch 1, sk st, puff 3 in next st from Rnd 3, ch 1, sk st] around, join to first fpdtr made, do not fasten off.

<16 fpdtr, 16 puff 3, 32 ch-1 sp>

Round 5: C2

In any ch-1 sp, make a standing 2 sc in each ch-1 sp around, join to first sc made, fasten off. *<64 sc>*

Round 6: C3

Around any fpdtr from Rnd 4, make a standing [fptr around fpdtr from Rnd 4, dc in next 4 sts] around, join to first fptr made, do not fasten off. *<16 fptr, 64 dc>*

Round 7: C3

Ch 1 (doesn't count as st), sc in each st around, join to first sc made, fasten off.

<80 sc>

Round 8: C4

In first sc made in prev rnd, make a standing [tr2cl in st, ch 3, sk st, sc in next 2 sts, ch 3, sk st] around, join to first tr2cl made, do not fasten off. *<16 tr2cl, 32 ch-3 sp, 32 sc>*

Round 9: C4

(Beg tr2cl, ch 7, tr2cl) in same st as join, (tr2cl, ch 7, tr2cl) in each cl around, join to first cl made, do not fasten off. *<32 tr2cl, 16 ch-7 sp>*

Round 10: C4

Ch 1 (doesn't count as st), sc in same st as join, 7 sc in ch-7 sp, sk st, [sc in next st, 7 sc in ch-7 sp, sk st] around, join to first sc made, fasten off. *<128 sc>*

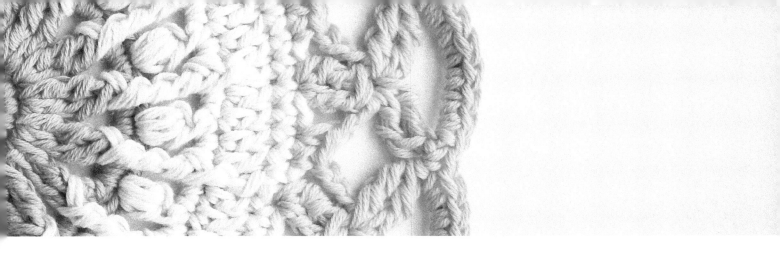

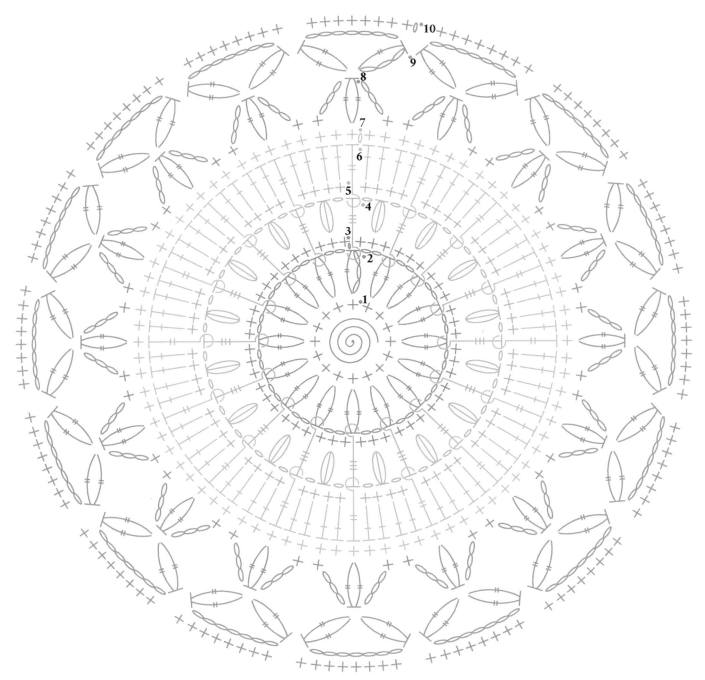

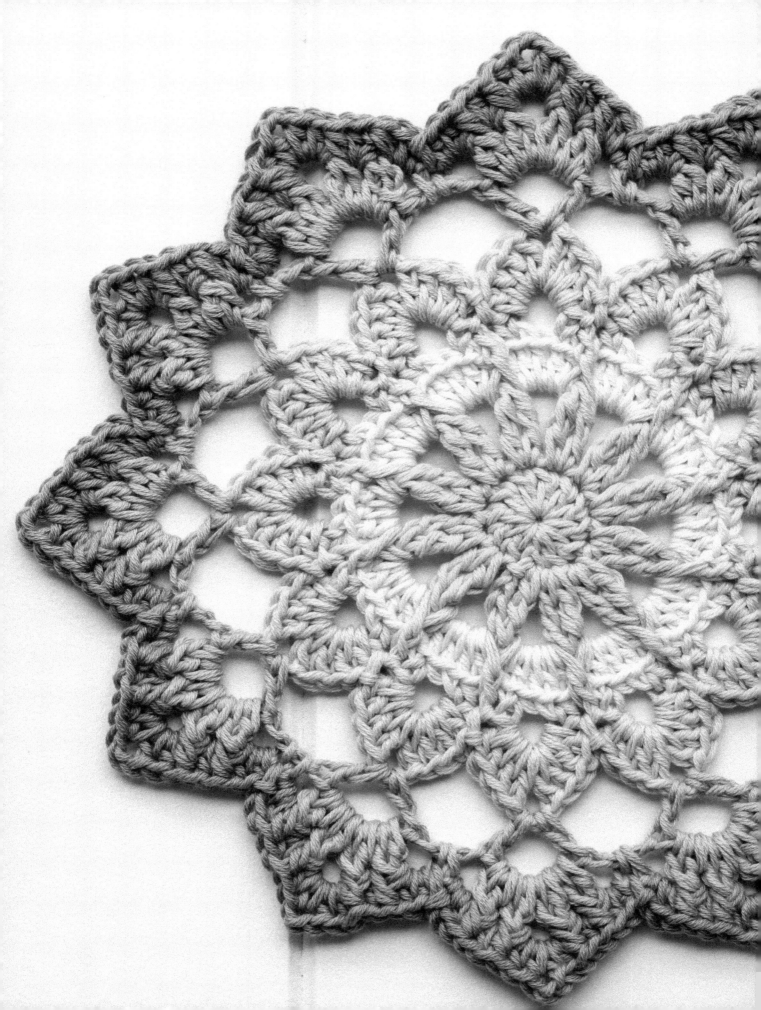

EXCITEMENT

MANDALA

noun. an excited state or condition

There is no excitement quite like that of a crocheter buying more yarn

FINISHED SIZE

21cm/8.2in unblocked

MATERIALS

Naturals Organic Cotton
One ball of each

Colour 1 7175 Citron

Colour 2 7173 Bone

Colour 3 7187 Flax

Colour 4 7182 Pink Clay

Colour 5 7189 Rosewood

US G-6 / UK 8 / (4mm) hook

Yarn Needle

Scissors

Stitch Marker

NOTES & TIPS

Round 6

Sometimes, you can start your standing stitches without a knot already on your hook, this gives the piece an even more uniform, invisible join. But in the instance where you use the same colour in the following round, I recommend using a knot for standing stitches.

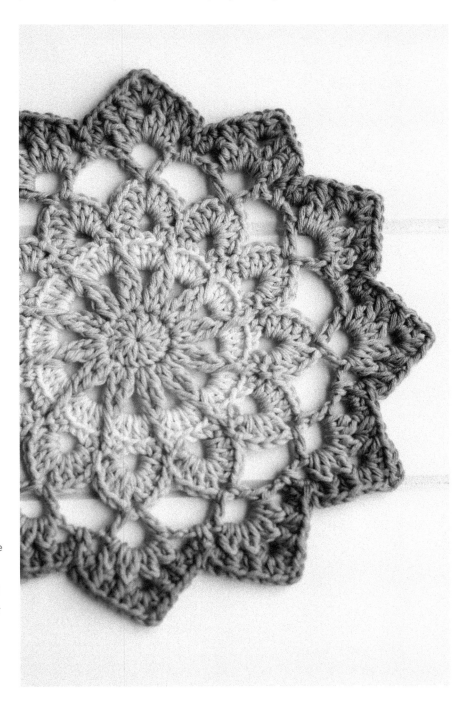

I am excited for all of the good things to come.

affirmation

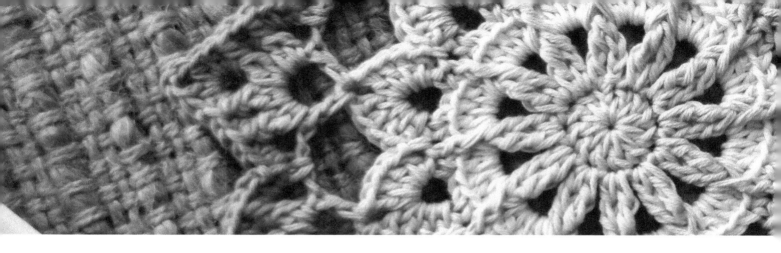

Round 1: C1

Make a MR, or (ch 4, join to first ch to form ring), ch 3 (counts as dc), 11 dc in ring, join to top of ch-3, do not fasten off. *<12 dc>*

Round 2: C1

Beg tr2cl, ch 2 in same st as join, (tr2cl, ch 2) in each st around, join to first cl made, fasten off. *<12 tr2cl, 12 ch-2 sp>*

Round 3: C2

In any ch-2 sp, make a standing 5 dc in each ch-2 sp around, join to first dc made, fasten off. *<60 dc>*

Round 4: C3

Around any cl from Rnd 2, make a standing [fpdc around cl from Rnd 2, sk next st, blo sc in next st, ch 4, sk st, blo sc in next st, sk st] around, join to first fpdc made, do not fasten off. *<12 fpdc, 24 bloc sc, 12 ch-4 sp>*

Round 5: C3

In any ch-4 sp, make a standing (4 dc, ch 2, 4 dc) in ch-4 sp, sk st, sl st in fpdc, sk st] around, fasten off. *<96 dc, 12 sl st, 12 ch-2 sp>*

Round 6: C4

In any ch-2 sp, make a standing [(dc, ch 4, dc) in ch-2 sp, ch 3, sk 9 sts] around, join to first dc made, do not fasten off. *<24 dc, 12 ch-4 sp, 12 ch-3 sp>*

Round 7: C4

Sl st to ch-4 sp, (beg dc2cl, ch 1, dc2cl, ch 3, dc2cl, ch 1, dc2cl) in same sp, ch 2, sk st, sc in ch-3 sp, ch 2, [(dc2cl, ch 1, dc2cl, ch 3, dc2cl, ch 1, dc2cl) in ch-4 sp, ch 2, sk st, sc in ch-3 sp, ch 2, sk st] around, join to first cl made, fasten off. *<12 sc, 24 ch-2 sp, 12 ch-3 sp, 24 ch-1 sp, 48 dc2cl>*

Round 8: C5

In any ch-3 sp, make a standing [(2 hdc, ch-2, 2 hdc) in ch-3 sp, fphdc around cl, hdc in ch-1 sp, fphdc around cl, 2 hdc in ch-2 sp, sl st in sc, 2 hdc in ch-2 sp, fphdc around cl, hdc in ch-1 sp, fphdc around cl] around, join to first hdc made, fasten off. *<12 sl st, 120 hdc, 48 fphdc>*

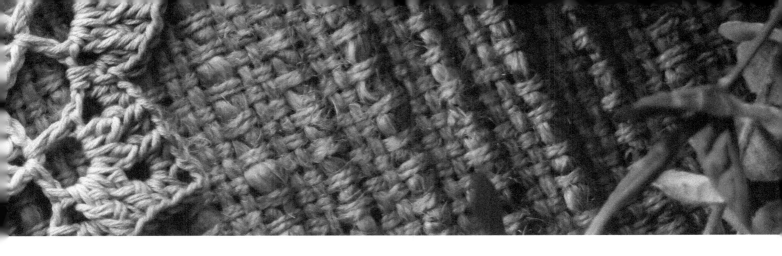

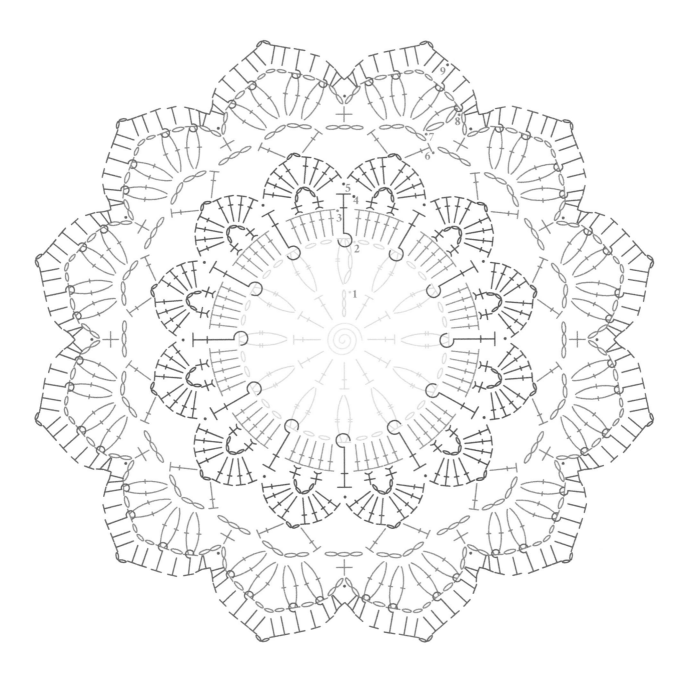

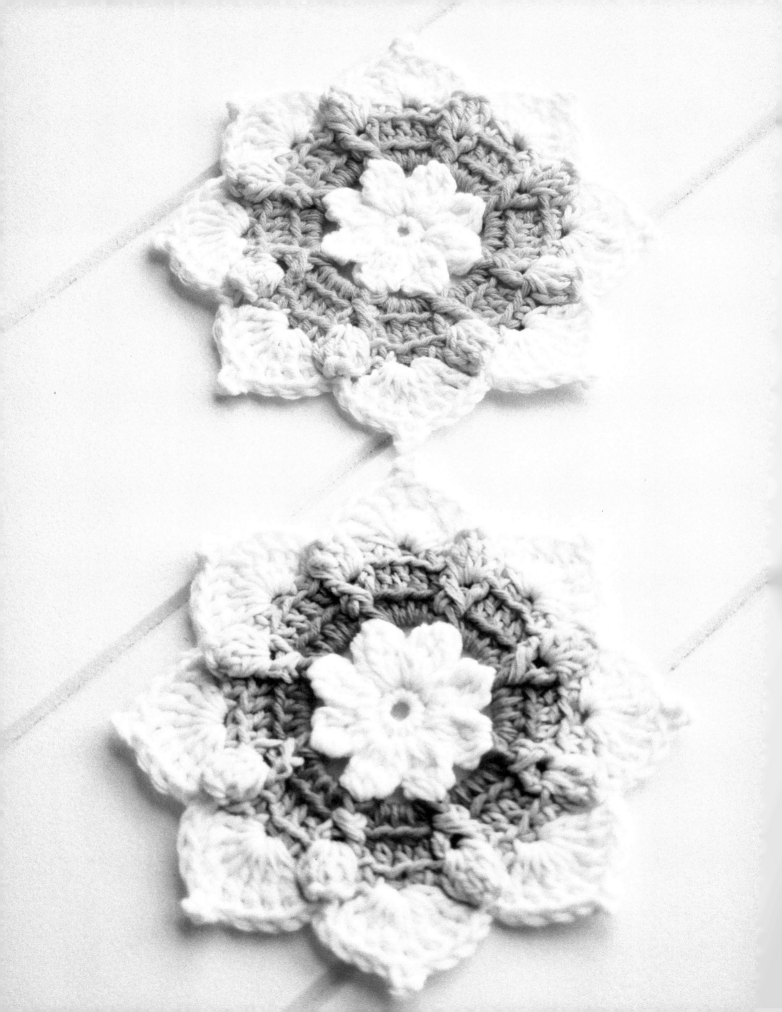

EXPLORATION

MANDALA

noun. an act or instance of exploring or investigating; examination

Crocheters do this when they're looking for yarn they know they have 'somewhere' in their stash....

FINISHED SIZE

14.5cm/5.7in unblocked

MATERIALS

Naturals Organic Cotton
One ball of each

Colour 1 7168 Gypsum

Colour 2 7178 Papaya

Colour 3 7180 Coral

Colour 4 7174 Buttermilk

Colour 5 7201 Indigo Wash

Colour 6 7199 Deep Sea

Colour 7 7172 Peppermint

US G-6 / UK 8 / (4mm) hook

Yarn Needle

Scissors

NOTES & TIPS

Third Loop

Work in the loop behind the 'V' as stated.

Magic Ring

After Round 2, pull Magic Ring nice and tight, but not too tight, enough to keep all the stitches nice and uniform.

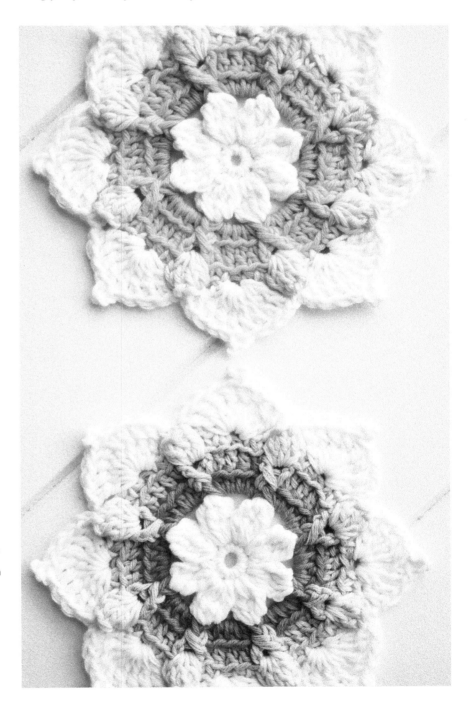

Exploration is curiosity put into action

Don Walsh

49

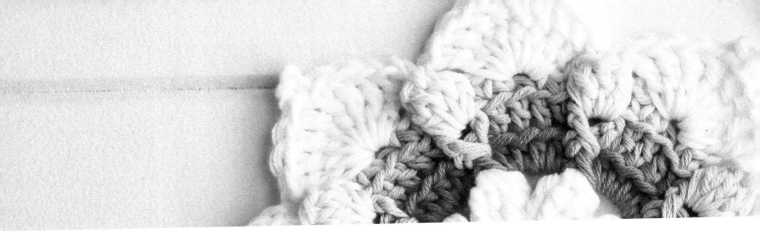

Round 1: C1

Make a MR, or (ch 4, join to first ch to form ring), ch 1 (doesn't count as st), 8 sc in ring, join to first sc, do not fasten off. *<8 sc>*

Round 2: C1

Beg tr4cl in same st as join, ch 3, (tr4cl, ch 3) in each st around, join to first cl made, fasten off. *<8 tr4cl, 8 ch-3 sp>*

Round 3: C2

Around any cl, make a standing [fphdc around cl, 4 hdc in ch-3 sp] around, join to first hdc made, fasten off. *<8 fphdc, 32 hdc>*

Round 4: C3

Around any fphdc, make a standing [(fpdc, ch 1, fpdc) around fphdc, blo hdc in next 4 sts] around, join to first fpdc made, fasten off. *<16 fpdc, 8 ch-1 sp, 32 blo hdc>*

Round 5: C4

In any ch-1 sp, make a standing [pop in ch-1 sp, ch-2, sk fpdc, blo sc in next 2 sts, ch 1, blo sc in next 2 sts, ch 2, sk fpdc] around, join to first pop made, fasten off. *<8 pop, 8 ch-1 sp, 32 blo sc, 16 ch-2 sp>*

Round 6: C1

In any pop, make a standing [sc in pop, ch 1, sk (ch-2 sp, 2 sc), (4 tr, picot 3, 4 tr) in ch-1 sp, ch 1, sk (2 sc, ch-2 sp)] around, join to first sc made, fasten off. *<64 tr, 8 picot 3, 8 sc, 16 ch-1 sp>*

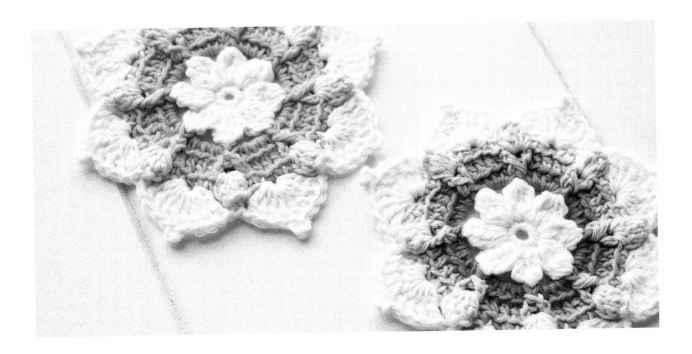

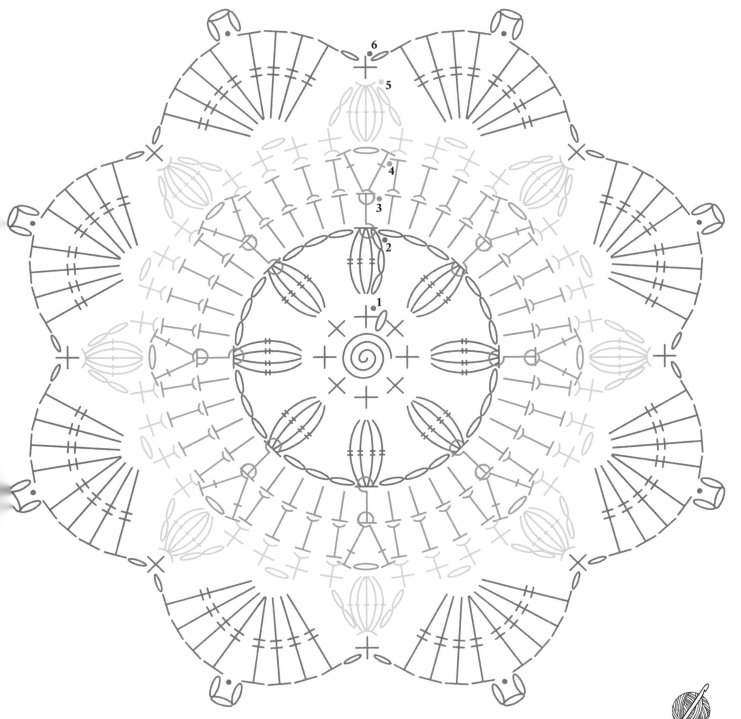

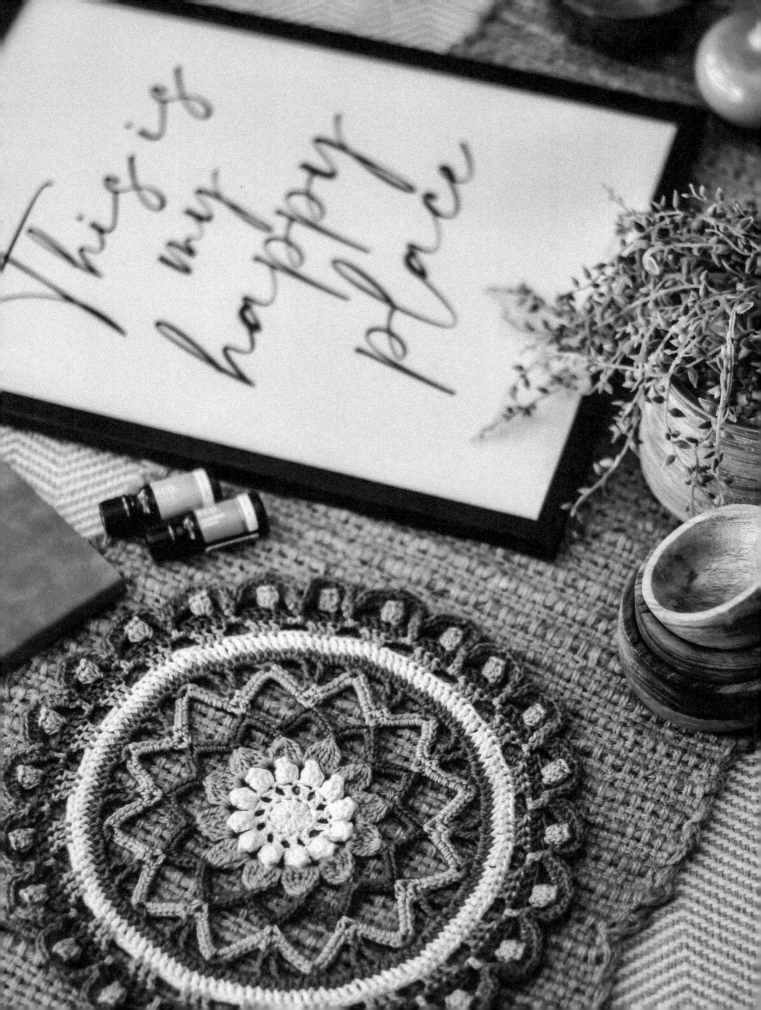

FEARLESS

MANDALA

adjective. without fear; bold or brave; intrepid
A crocheter is fearless, especially when it comes to frogging.

FINISHED SIZE

30cm/11.8in unblocked

MATERIALS

Naturals Bamboo & Cotton
One ball of each

Colour 1 7128 Ecru
Colour 2 7147 Nutmeg
Colour 3 7161 Umber
Colour 4 7144 Surf
Colour 5 7152 Indigo

US E/4; UK 9; (3.5mm) hook
Yarn Needle
Scissors

NOTES & TIPS

Clusters

Pay attention to your placement of the cluster stitches in Round 4. Note that half is done on either side of the popcorn stitch.

Magic Ring

After Round 2, pull Magic Ring nice and tight, but not too tight, enough to keep all the stitches nice and uniform.

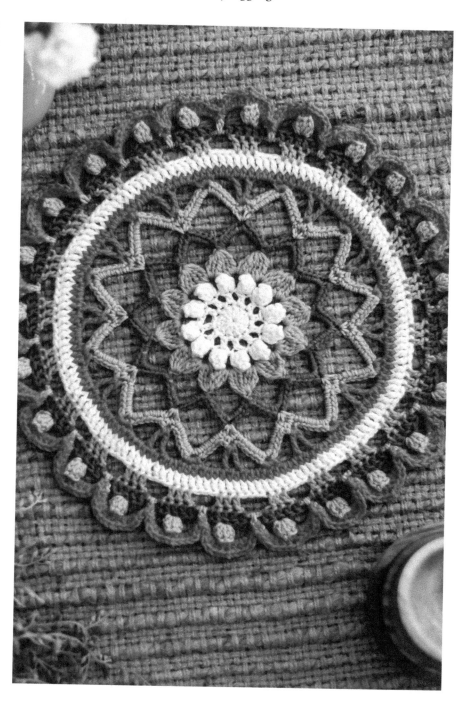

Once you become fearless, life becomes limitless.

Nishant Patel & Mit Bhatt

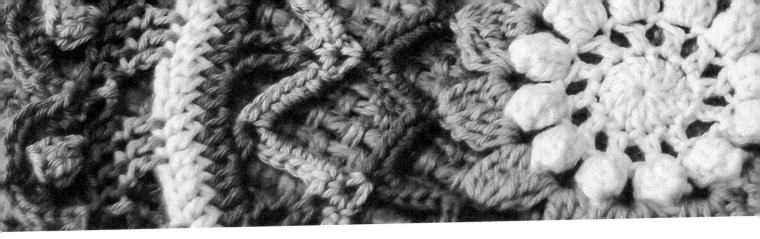

Round 1: C1

Make a MR, or ch 4, join to first ch to form ring, ch 3 (counts as dc), 11 dc in ring, join with sl st to top of ch-3, do not fasten off. *<12 dc>*

Round 2: C1

Ch 4 (counts as dc + ch 1), (dc, ch 1) in each st around, join with sl st to 3rd ch, do not fasten off. *<12 dc, 12 ch-1 sp>*

Round 3: C1

Beg pop in same st as join, ch 3, sk ch-sp, [pop in st, ch 3, sk ch-sp] around, join to first pop made, fasten off. *<12 pop, 12 ch-3 sp>*

Round 4: C2

In any ch-3 sp before pop, make a standing [tr6cl (3 legs on one side of the pop and 3 legs on the other), ch 8] around, join to first tr6cl made, fasten off. *<12 tr6cl, 12 ch-8 sp>*

Round 5: C3

In any cl, make a standing [fpsc around cl, (5 sc, ch 2, 5 sc) in ch-8 sp] around, join to first fpsc made, fasten off. *<12 fpsc, 120 sc, 12 ch-2 sp>*

Round 6: C4

Make a standing [(sc, ch 2, sc) in ch-2 sp, ch 10] around, join to first sc made, do not fasten off. *<24 sc, 12 ch-10 sp, 12 ch-2 sp>*

Round 7: C4

Ch 1 (doesn't count as st), [(sc, ch 2, sc) in ch-2 sp, sk st, (6 sc, ch 2, 6 sc) in ch-10 sp, sk st] around, join to first sc made, fasten off.

<168 sc, 24 ch-2 sp>

Round 8: C5

Make a standing [3 sc in higher ch-2 sp, ch 3, (tr, ch 1, tr) in lower ch-2 sp, ch 3] around, join to first sc made, do not fasten off. *<36 sc, 24 tr, 12 ch-1 sp, 24 ch-3 sp, 12 ch-1 sp>*

Round 9: C5

Ch 3 (counts a dc), dc in next 2 sts, 3 dc in ch-3 sp, dc in next st, dc in ch-sp, dc in next st, 3 dc in ch-3 sp, [dc in next 3 sts, 3 dc in ch-3 sp, dc in next st, dc in ch-sp, dc in next st, 3 dc in ch-3 sp] around, join to top of ch-3, fasten off. *<144 dc>*

Round 10: C1

Make a fpdc around first dc made in prev rnd, fpdc around each st around, join to first fpdc made, fasten off. *<144 fpdc>*

Round 11: C2

In first fpdc made, make a standing dc, dc in next 2 sts, ch 3, sk 3 sts, [dc in next 3 sts, ch 3, sk 3 sts] around, join to first dc made, fasten off. *<72 dc, 24 ch-3 sp>*

Round 12: C3

In first dc made in prev rnd, make a standing dc in st, dc in next 2 sts, (dc, ch 2, dc) in ch-3 sp, [dc in next 3 sts, (dc, ch 2, dc) in ch-3 sp] around, join to first dc made, fasten off. *<120 dc, 24 ch-2 sp>*

Round 13: C4

In any middle dc, make a standing [pop in middle dc from Rnd 12, ch 5, sc into ch-3 sp

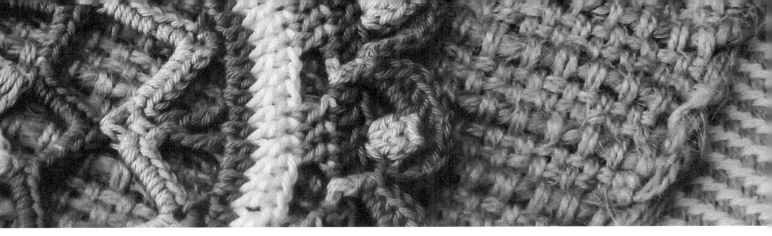

from Rnd 11, ch 5] around, join to first pop made, fasten off. *<24 pop, 24 sc, 48 ch-5 sp>*

Round 14: C5

Around any sc, make a standing [fpsc around sc, (2 hdc, 3 dc) in ch-5 sp, (dc, ch 2, dc) in pop, (3 dc, 2 hdc) in ch-5 sp] around, join to first fpsc made, fasten off. *<96 hdc, 24 fpsc, 192 dc, 24 ch-2 sp>*

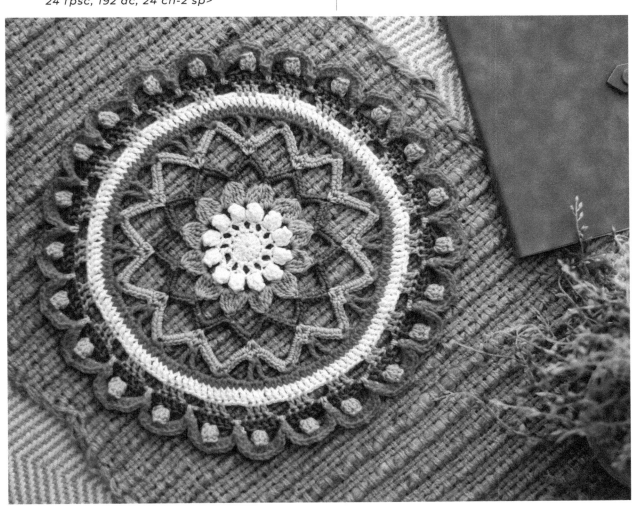

FEARLESS

MANDALA

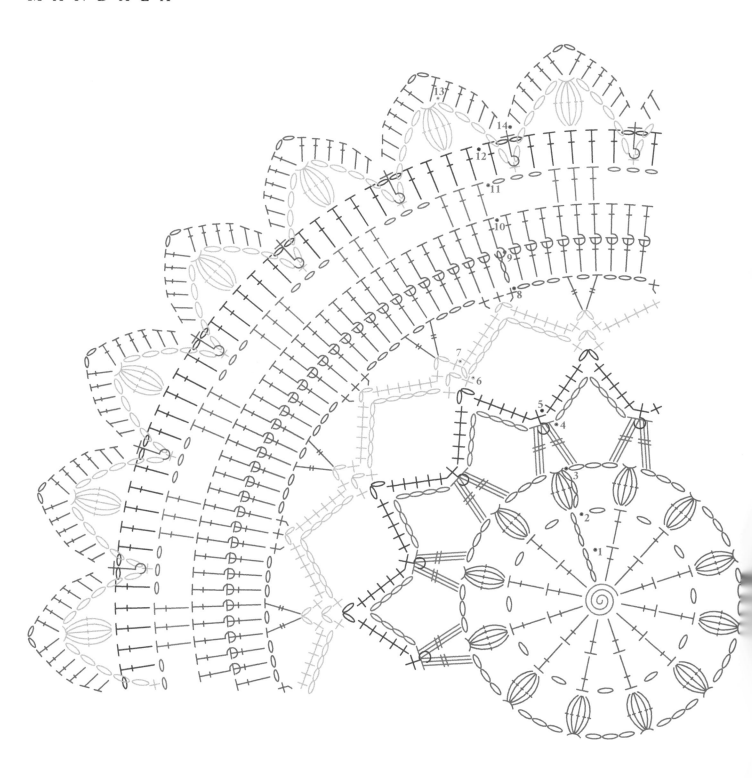

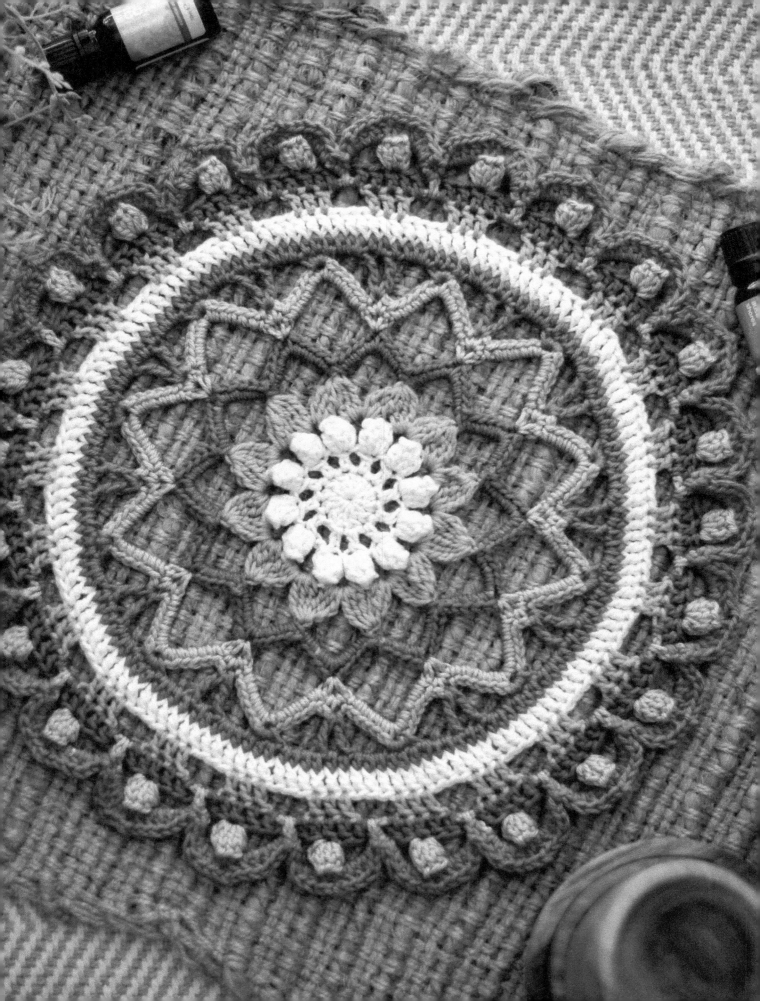

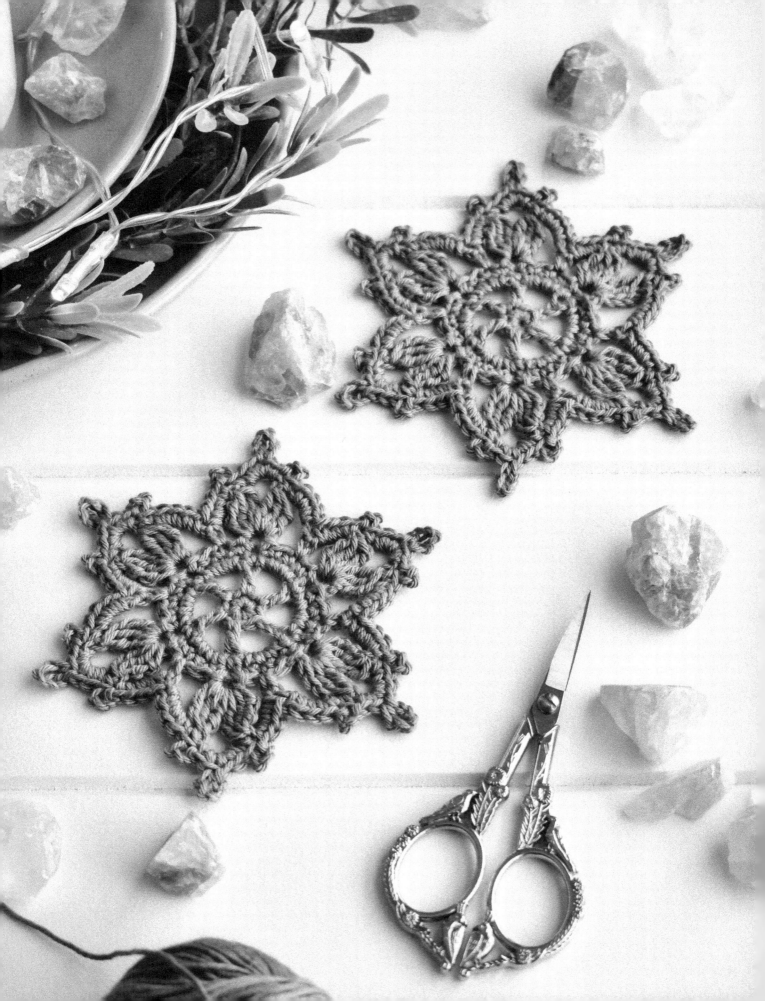

FOCUS
MANDALA

noun. close attention or concentration
Crocheters need to do this in order to avoid frogging.

FINISHED SIZE

11cm/4.3in unblocked

MATERIALS

Naturals Bamboo & Cotton
One ball

Colour 1 7126 Spring Green

US E/4; UK 9; (3.5mm) hook
Yarn Needle
Scissors

NOTES & TIPS

Blocking

Depending on what yarn you use, this little motif may need a block to showcase its picots.

Magic Ring

After Round 2, pull Magic Ring nice and tight, but not too tight, enough to keep all the stitches nice and uniform

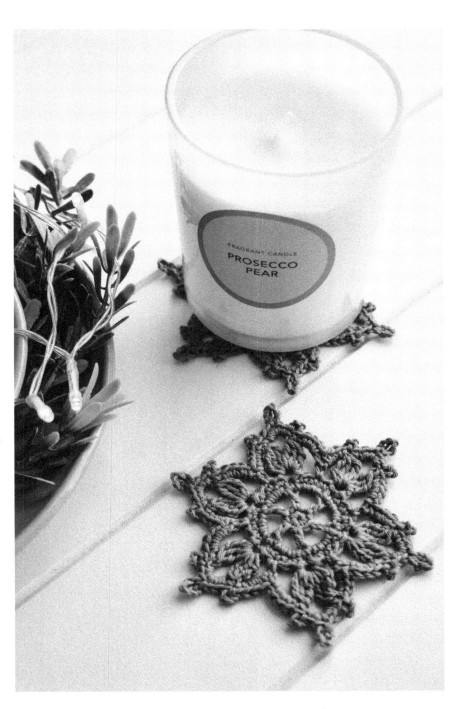

Where focus goes, energy flows. And where energy flows, whatever you're focusing on grows.
Tony Robbins

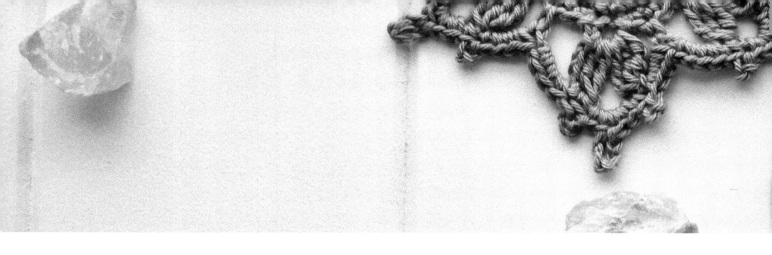

Round 1:

Make a MR, or (ch 3, join to first ch to form ring), ch 1 (doesn't count as st here and throughout), 6 sc in ring, join to first sc made. *<6 sc>*

Round 2:

Ch 6 (counts as dc + ch 3), (dc, ch 3) in each st around, join to top of 3rd ch.

<6 dc, 6 ch-3 sp>

Round 3:

Ch 1, sc in same st as join, 3 sc in ch-3 sp, [sc in st, 3 sc in ch-3 sp] around, join to first sc made. *<24 sc>*

Round 4:

Ch 4, sl st in same st as join, sc in next 3 sts, [(sl st, ch 4, sl st) in next st, sc in next 3 sts]

around, join in same st as Rnd 3 join. *<18 sc, 12 sl st, 6 ch-4 sp>*

Round 5:

Sl st to ch-4 sp, (beg tr3cl, ch 3, tr3cl) in same sp, ch 4, sk sc, sc in next st, ch 4, sk next st, [(tr3cl, ch 3, tr3cl) in ch-4 sp, ch 4, sk next sc, sc in next st, ch 4, sk next sc st] around, join to top of beg tr3cl

<12 tr3cl, 6 sc, 6 ch-3 sp, 12 ch-4 sp>

Round 6:

Ch 1, [(sc, picot 3) in same st as join, (2 sc, picot 5, 2 sc) in ch-3 sp, (sc, picot 3) in next st, 4 sc in each of next 2 ch-4 sps] around, join to first sc made, fasten off.

<84 sc, 12 picot 3, 6 picot 5>

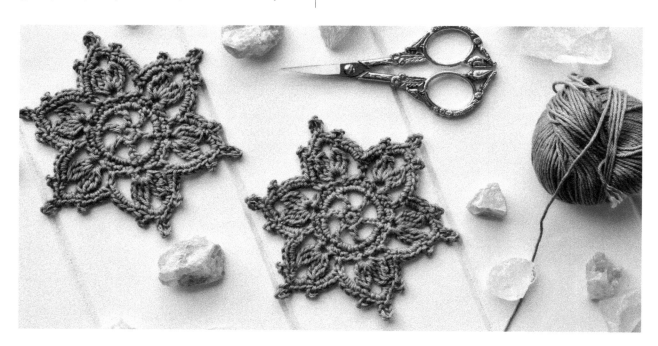

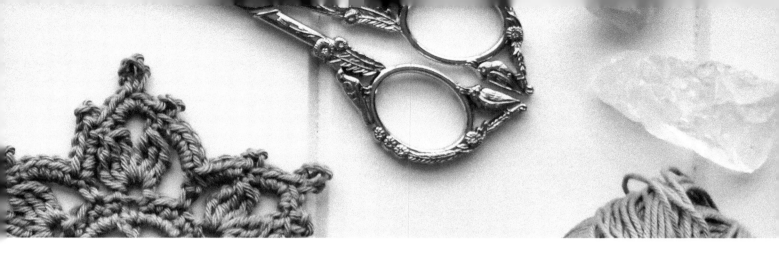

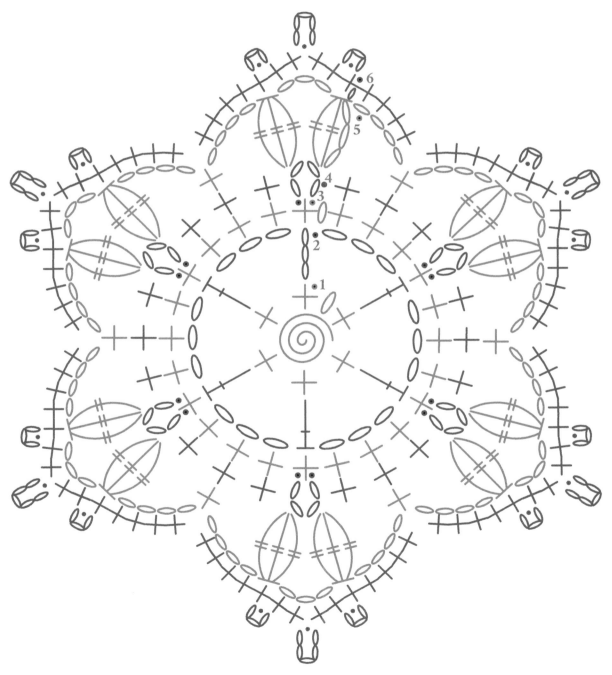

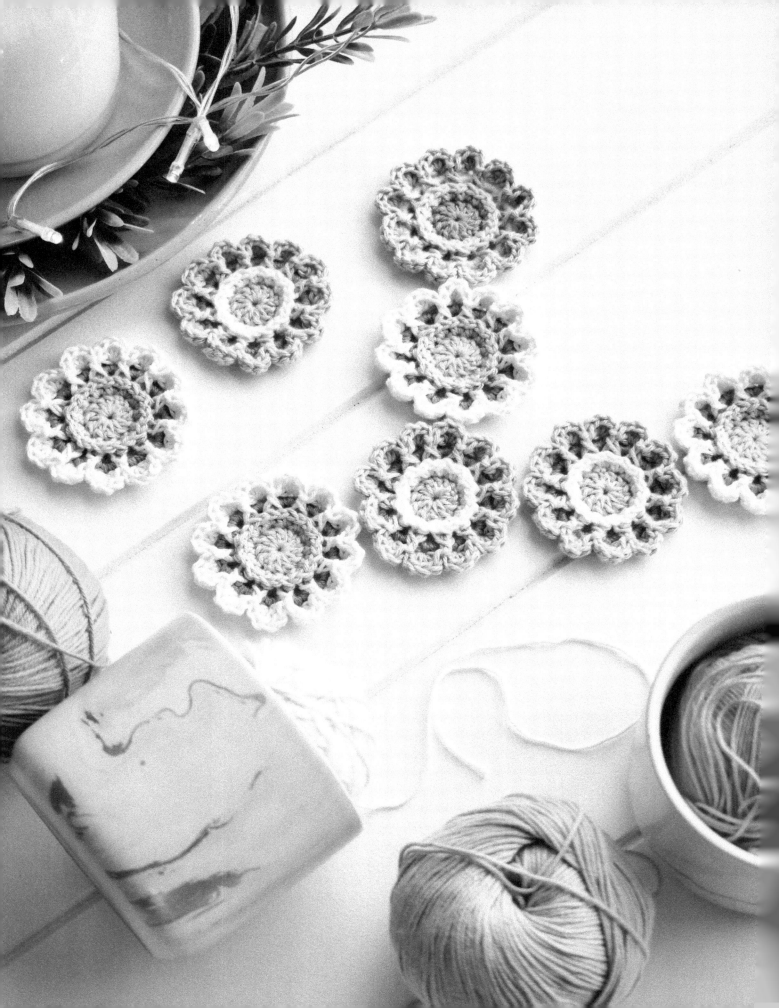

GOODNESS

MANDALA

noun. the state or quality of being good; moral excellence; virtue

The goodness that comes along with crocheting is the friendships that form for life.

FINISHED SIZE

6.5cm/2.5in unblocked

MATERIALS

Naturals Bamboo & Cotton
One ball of each

Colour 1 7128 Ecru
Colour 2 7162 Powder Blue
Colour 3 7165 Rose
Colour 4 7154 Pumice

US E-4 / UK 9 / (3.5mm) hook
Yarn Needle
Scissors

NOTES & TIPS

Colour Placement

Have fun playing around with colour in this pattern. The pattern has the guides for colour changes, so just make note when to start and finish each one.

Round 3

Fold round 2 slightly forward, you will see 2 prominent loops that stick out. This is where you will make your slip stitch. If you find it too difficult, you could slip stitch into the 3rd loop instead.

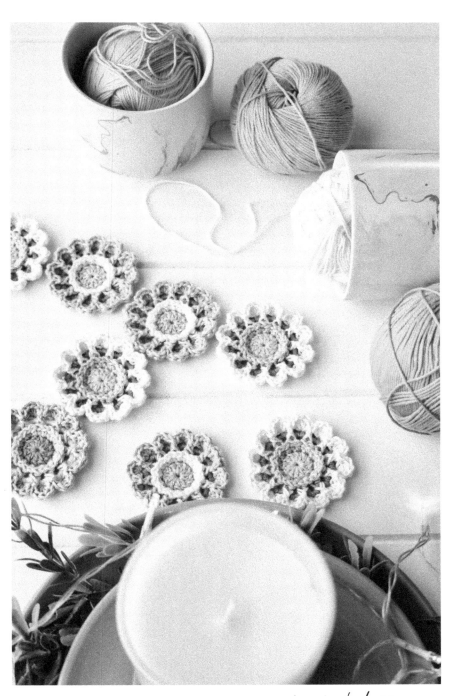

Goodness is about character - integrity, honesty, kindness, generosity, moral courage, and the like. More than anything else, it is about how we treat other people.
Dennis Prager

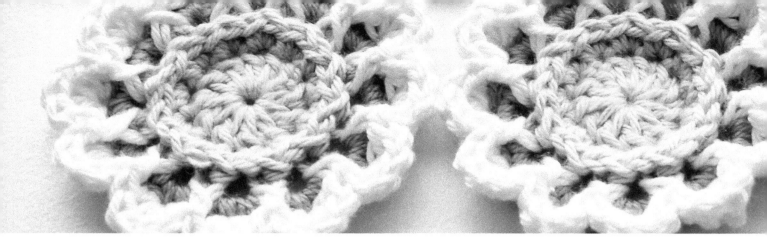

Round 1: C1

Make a MR, or (ch 4, join to first ch to form ring), ch 3 (counts as dc), 11 dc in ring, join to top of ch-3, fasten off. *<12 dc>*

Round 2: C2

In any st, make a standing (dc, sc) in each st around, join to first dc made, fasten off. *<12 dc, 12 sc>*

Round 3: C3 – *Fold Rnd 2 slightly forward, the loops of dc post are on the back of the st*

In any dc, [sl st into both loops of dc post from Rnd 2, ch 2] around, sl st to same st as first sl st made, do not fasten off. *<12 sl st, 12 ch-2 sp>*

Round 4: C3

3 sc in each ch-2 sp around, skipping sl st, join to first sc made, fasten off. *<36 sc>*

Round 5: C4

Around any sl st, make a standing [fpsc around sl st from Rnd 3, sk st, 5 dc in next st on Rnd 4, sk st] around, join to first fpsc made, fasten off. *<12 fpsc, 60 dc>*

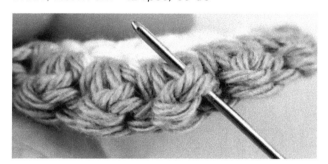

RND 3 - PHOTOS OF LOOPS TO WORK INTO
WRONG SIDE SHOWING (BACK)

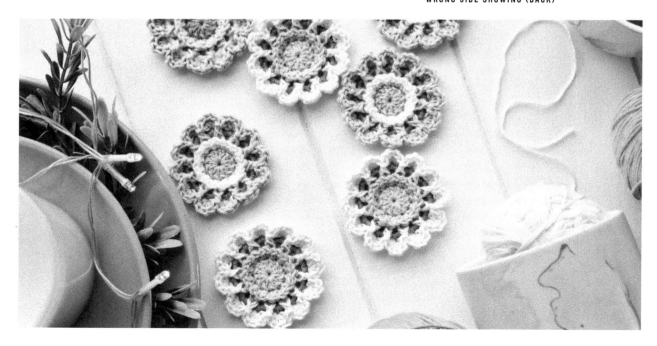

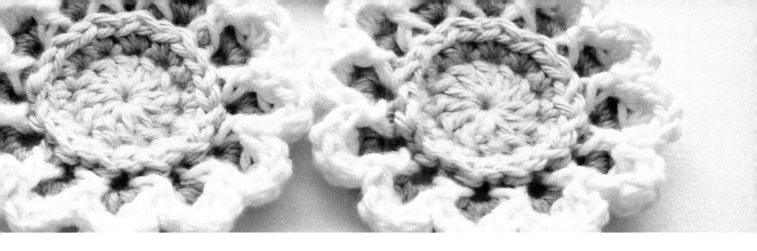

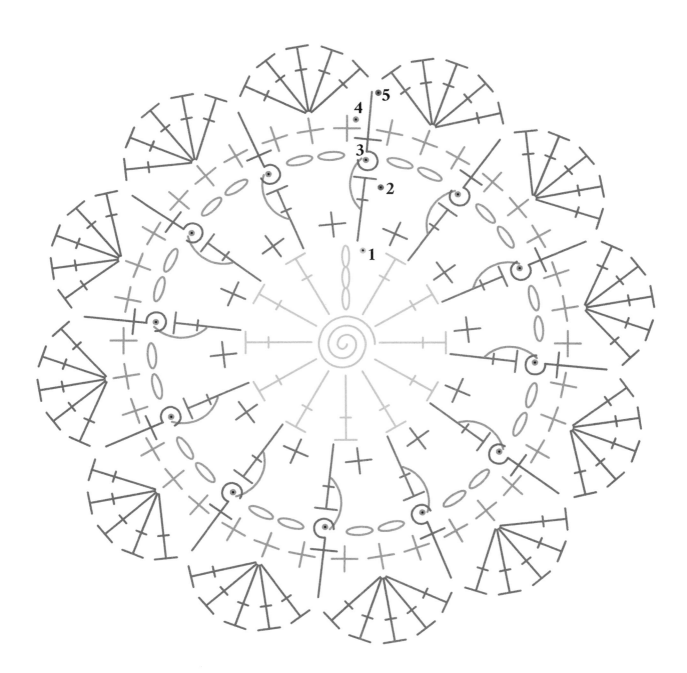

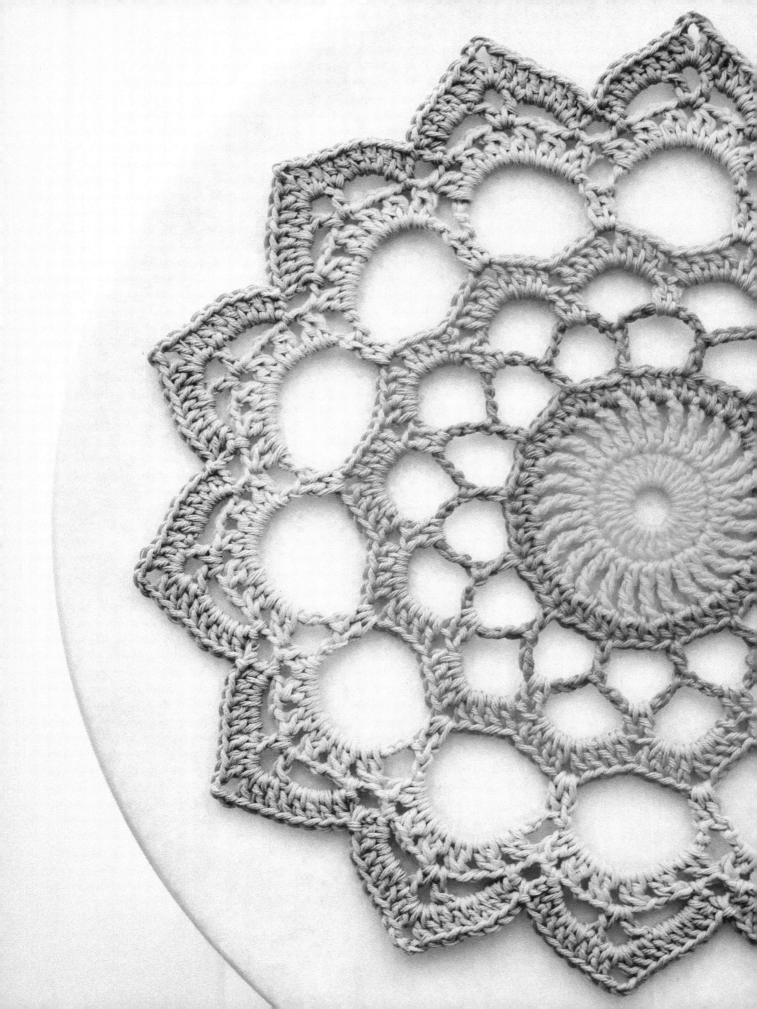

GRATITUDE

M A N D A L A

noun. the quality or feeling of being grateful or thankful

What crocheters feel when they see the postman after probably stalking them for too long.

FINISHED SIZE

14.5cm/5.7in unblocked

MATERIALS

Naturals Organic Cotton
One ball of each

Colour 1 7181 Carrot
Colour 2 7179 Flamingo
Colour 3 7185 Amethyst
Colour 4 7198 Azure
Colour 5 7191 Jade
Colour 6 7171 Leaf

US G/6 UK 8 (4mm) hook
Yarn Needle
Scissors

NOTES & TIPS

Stitch Count

Triple check the Round 1 stitch count - don't do what I did and just thought 'Oh yeah, that looks about it'...turns out I had completely missed like 12 stitches so my piece didn't lie flat.

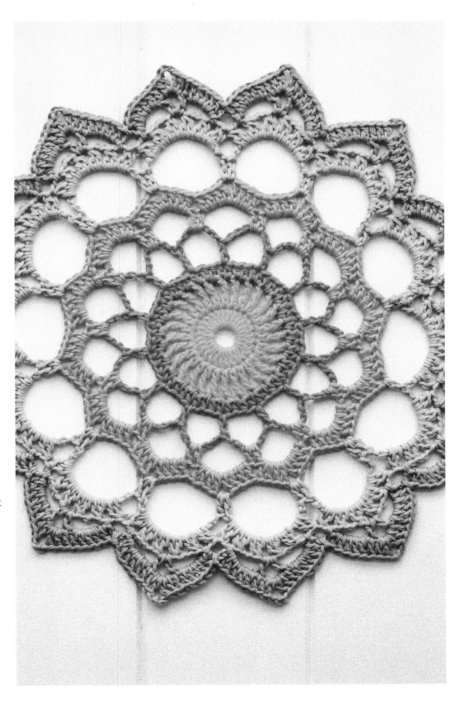

Helps you see what is there instead of what is not.

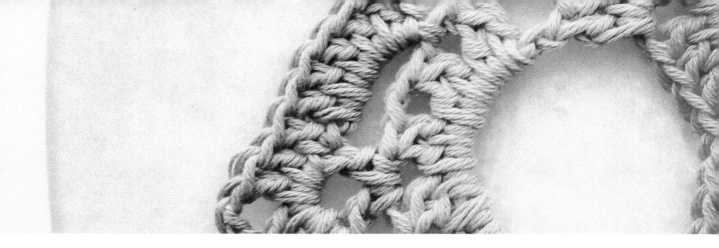

Round 1: C1

Make a MR, or (ch 14, join to first ch to form ring), ch 3 (counts as dc here and through-out), 27 dc in ring, join to top of ch-3, do not fasten off. *<28 dc>*

Round 2: C1

Ch 5 (counts as tr + ch 1), (tr, ch 1) in each st around, join to fourth ch, fasten off. *<28 tr, 28 ch-1 sp>*

Round 3: C2

In any tr st, make a standing [hdc in st, hdc in ch-1 sp] around, join to first hdc made, do not fasten off. *<56 hdc>*

Round 4: C2

Ch 10 (counts as dc + ch 7), sk 3 sts, [dc in next st, ch 7, sk 3 sts] around, join to ch-3, fasten off. *<14 dc, 14 ch-7 sp>*

Round 5: C3

In any ch-7 sp, make a standing [2 dc in ch-7 sp, ch 6, sk st] around, join to first dc made, do not fasten off. *<28 dc, 14 ch-6 sp>*

Round 6: C3

Sl st to ch-6 sp, ch 3, (3 dc, ch 2, 4 dc) in same sp, sk 2 sts, [(4 dc, ch 2, 4 dc) in ch-6 sp, sk 2 sts] around, join to top of third ch, fasten off. *<112 dc, 14 ch-2 sp>*

Round 7: C4

In any ch-2 sp, make a standing [2 dc in ch-2 sp, ch 12, sk 8 sts] around, join to first dc made, do not fasten off. *<28 dc, 14 ch-12 sp>*

Round 8: C4

Sl st in next st and next 2 ch-sts, sl st in ch-12 sp, beg dc2cl, ch 2, [(dc2cl, ch 2) 4 times, dc2cl] in same sp, sk 2 sts, *([dc2cl, ch 2] 5 times, dc2cl) in ch-12 sp, sk 2 sts; rep from * around, join to first cl made, fasten off. *<84 dc2cl, 70 ch-2 sp>*

Round 9: C5

In any middle ch-2 sp, make a standing [(dc, ch 3, dc) in middle ch-2 sp, ch 6, sk next (st, ch-2 sp, st), sl st in next ch-2 sp, ch 4, sk 2 sts, sl st in next ch-2 sp, ch 6, sk next (st, ch-2 sp, st)] around, join to first dc made, do not fasten off. *<28 sl st, 28 dc, 14 ch-3 sp, 28 ch-6 sp, 14 ch-4 sp>*

Round 10: C5

Ch 3, (2 dc, ch 3, 2 dc) in ch-3 sp, dc in next st, 5 dc in ch-6 sp, sk sl st, sl st in ch-4 sp, sk sl st, 5 dc in ch-6 sp, [dc in next st, (2 dc, ch 3, 2 dc) in ch-3 sp, dc in next st, 5 dc in ch-6 sp, sk sl st, sl st in ch-4 sp, sk sl st, 5 dc in ch-6 sp] around, join to top of ch-3, fasten off. *<224 dc, 14 ch-3 sp, 14 sl st>*

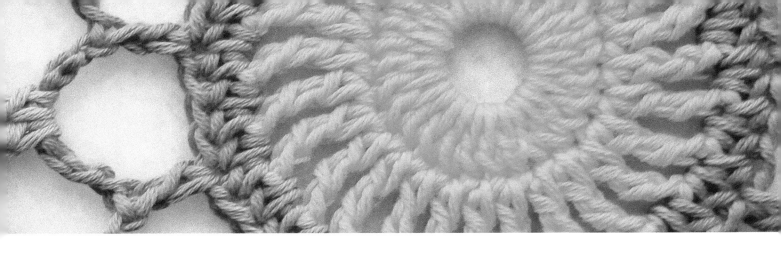

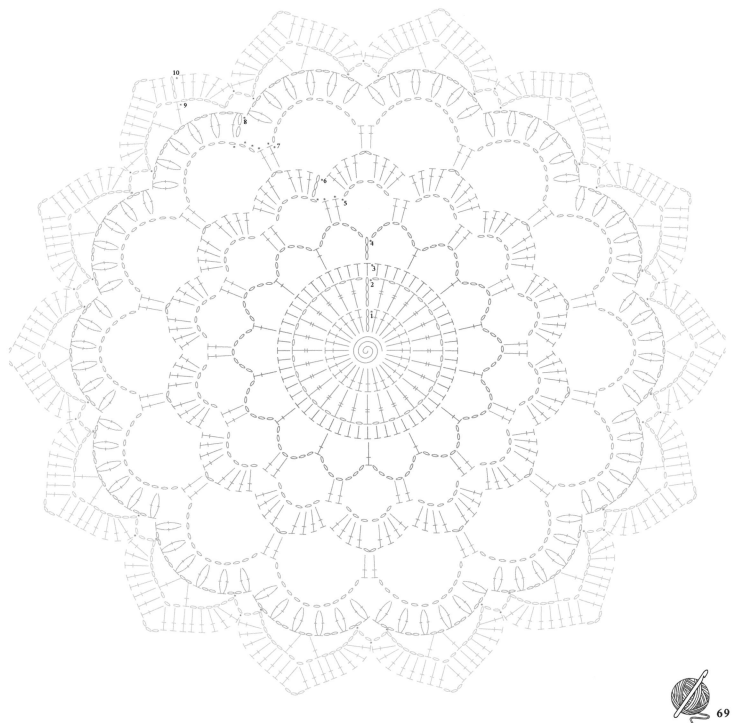

10
9
8
7
6
5
4
3
2
1

HAPPINESS

MANDALA

noun. an excited state or condition

What crocheters feel when they finish their current wip and weave in the very last end.

FINISHED SIZE

10cm/3.9in unblocked

MATERIALS

Naturals Bamboo & Cotton
One ball of each

Colour 1 7128 Ecru

Colour 2 7130 Apricot

Colour 3 7131 Peach

Colour 4 7132 Pale Pink

Colour 5 7133 Blush

US E/4; UK 9; (3.5mm) hook

Yarn Needle

Scissors

NOTES & TIPS

Round 5

Pay attention to where the hdc stitches are placed. Don't make a boo-boo and forget to skip the sc stitches.

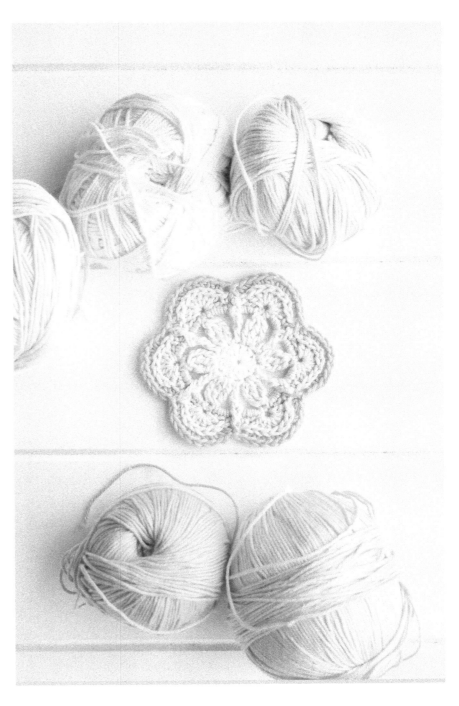

Happiness depends upon ourselves

Aristotle

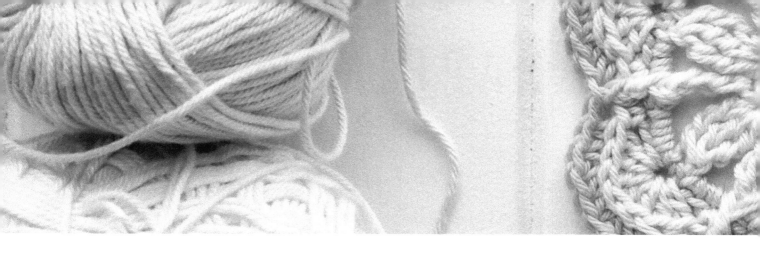

Round 1: C1

Make a MR, or (ch 4, join to first ch to form ring), ch 3 (counts as dc), 11 dc in ring, join to top of ch-3, do not fasten off. *<12 dc>*

Round 2: C1

Sl st to next st, beg tr3cl, ch 2, tr in next st, ch 2, [tr3cl in next st, ch 2, tr in next st, ch 2] around, join to first cl made, fasten off. *<6 tr3cl, 6 tr, 12 ch-2 sp>*

Round 3: C2

In any cl, make a standing [sc in cl, 3 sc in ch-2 sp, sc in tr, 3 sc in ch-2 sp] around, join to first sc made. Fasten off. *<48 sc>*

Round 4: C3

In sc made in cl, make a standing [7 dc in st, sk 2 sts, sc in next st, fpdc around tr from Rnd 2, sk st behind fpdc, sc in next st, sk 2 sts] around, join to first dc made. Fasten off. *<6 fpdc, 12 sc, 42 dc>*

Round 5: C1 - *Hdc sts are worked in third loop only, sk sc from Rnd 4.*

Make a standing [fpsc around fpdc, sk st, (hdc in next st, 2 hdc in next st) three times, hdc in next st, sk st] around, join to first fpsc made. Fasten off. *<6 fpsc, 60 hdc in 3rd loop>*

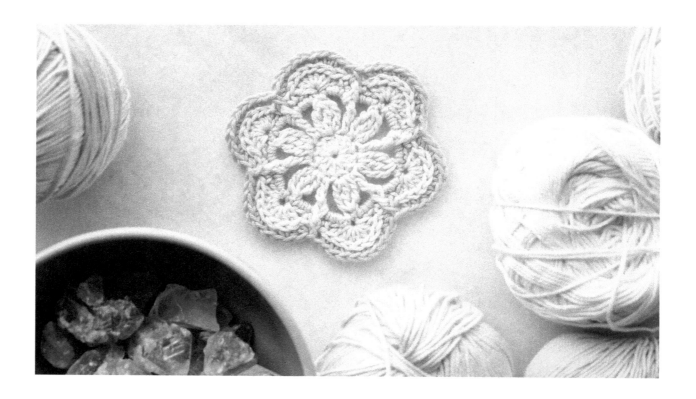

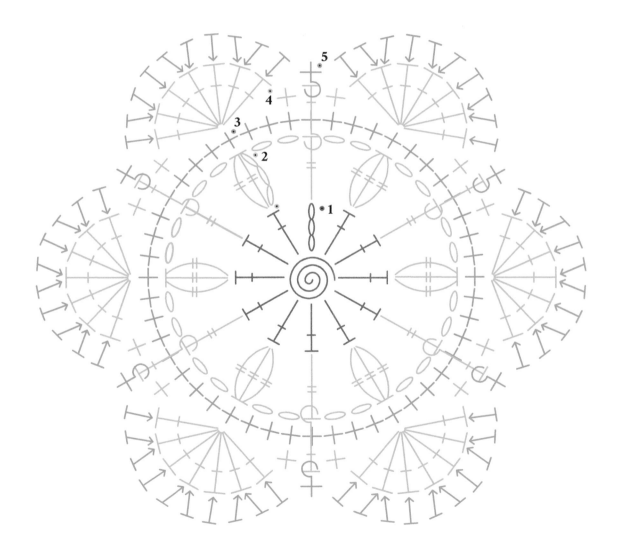

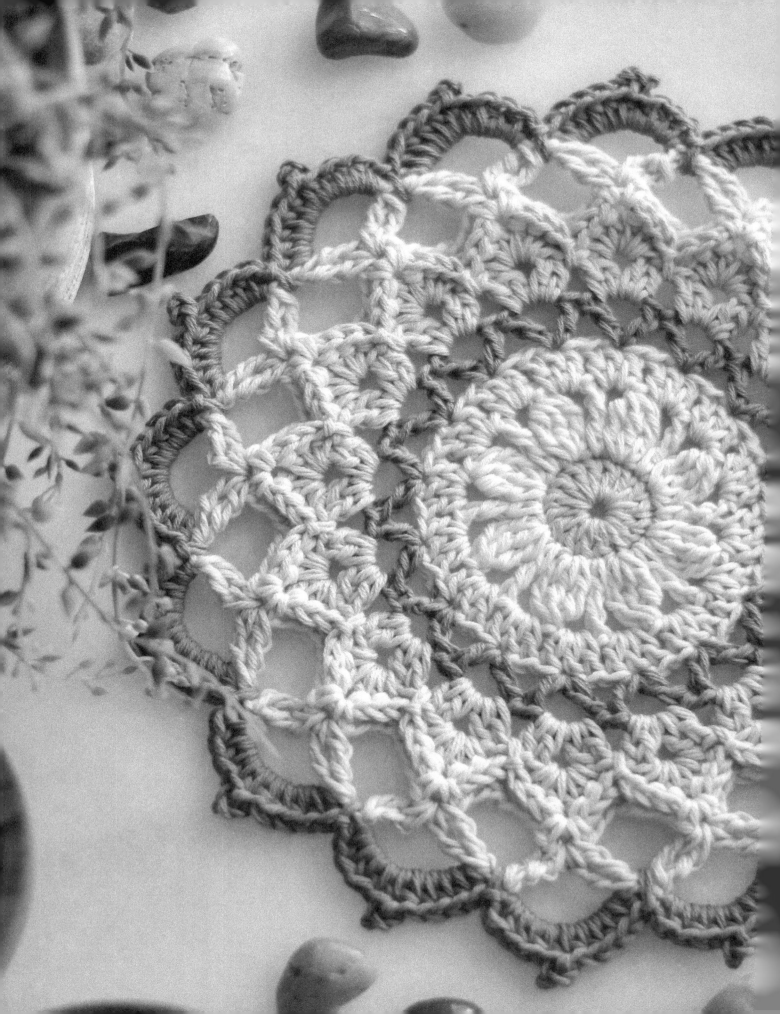

HONESTY

MANDALA

noun. truthfulness, sincerity or frankness

What you need in a crochet friend when you are unsure of your colour selection.

FINISHED SIZE

14.5cm/5.7in unblocked

MATERIALS

Naturals Organic Cotton
One ball of each

Colour 1 7187 Flax
Colour 2 7173 Bone
Colour 3 7195 Faded Denim
Colour 4 7200 Blue Dusk

US G/6 UK 8 (4mm) hook
Yarn Needle
Scissors

NOTES & TIPS

Attaching to a ring
This mandala would look gorgeous
attached to a ring in the picots only.
Are you feeling intrigued yet?
Are you going to try it?

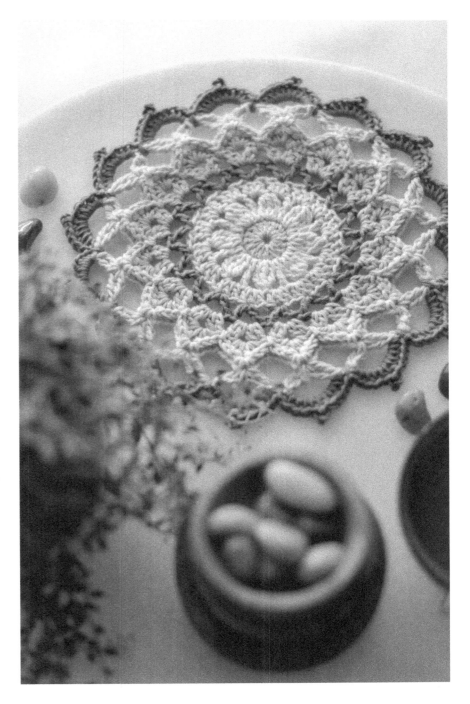

Never say sorry for being honest

Buddha

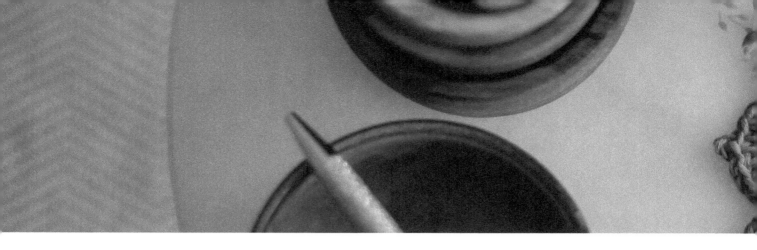

Round 1: C1

Make a MR, or (ch 6, join to first ch to form ring), ch 3 (counts as dc here and throughout), 15 dc in ring, join to top of ch-3, fasten off. *<16 dc>*

Round 2: C2

In any st, make a standing [tr in st, ch 2, tr3cl in next st, ch 2] around, join to first tr made, fasten off. *<8 tr, 8 tr3cl, 16 ch-2 sp>*

Round 3: C3

In any ch-2 sp, make a standing 3 dc in each ch-2 sp around, join to first dc made, fasten off. *<48 dc>*

Round 4: C4

In any middle dc, make a standing [(dc, ch 3, dc) in middle dc, sk 2 sts] around, join to first dc made, fasten off. *<32 dc, 16 ch-3 sp>*

Round 5: C1

In any ch-3 sp, make a standing [(2 dc, ch 2, 2 dc) in ch-3 sp, sk 2 sts] around, join to first dc made, do not fasten off. *<64 dc, 16 ch-2 sp>*

Round 6: C1

Sl st to ch-2 sp, ch 3 (counts as st), (2 dc, ch 2, 3 dc) in same sp, sk 2 sts, sl st in between the two sets of dc sts, sk 2 sts, [(3 dc, ch 2, 3 dc) in ch-2 sp, sk 2 sts, sl st in between the two sets of dc sts, sk 2 sts] around, join to top of ch 3, fasten off. *<96 dc, 16 ch-2 sp, 16 sl st>*

Round 7: C2

Starting at first dc made in prev rnd, make a standing [bpsc around each of next 3 sts, (sc, ch 2, sc) in ch-2 sp, bpsc around each of next 3 sts, ch 1, sk sl st] around, join to first bpsc made, fasten off. *<96 bpsc, 16 ch-1 sp, 32 sc, 16 ch-2 sp>*

Round 8: C3

In any ch-2 sp, make a standing [(tr2cl, ch 7, tr2cl) in ch-2 sp, sk 8 sts] around, join to first cl made, fasten off. *<32 tr2cl, 16 ch-7 sp>*

Round 9: C4

In any ch-7 sp, make a standing [(5 hdc, picot 3, 5 hdc) in ch-7 sp, sl st in between clusters] around, join to first sc made, fasten off. *<160 hdc, 16 picot 3, 16 sl st >*

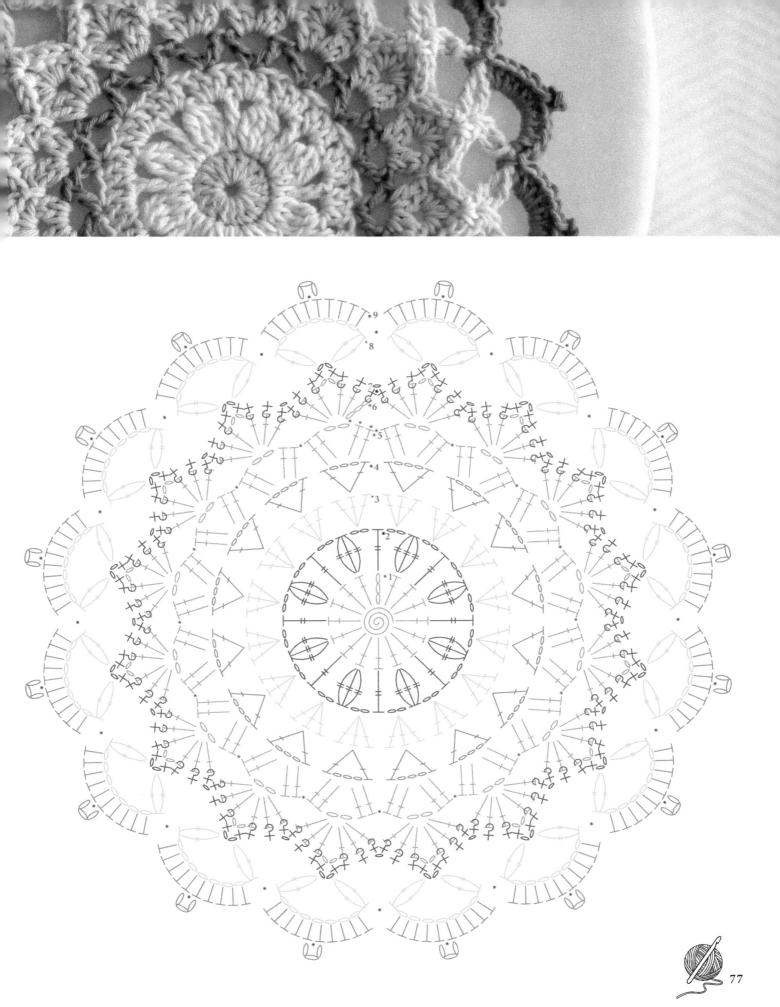

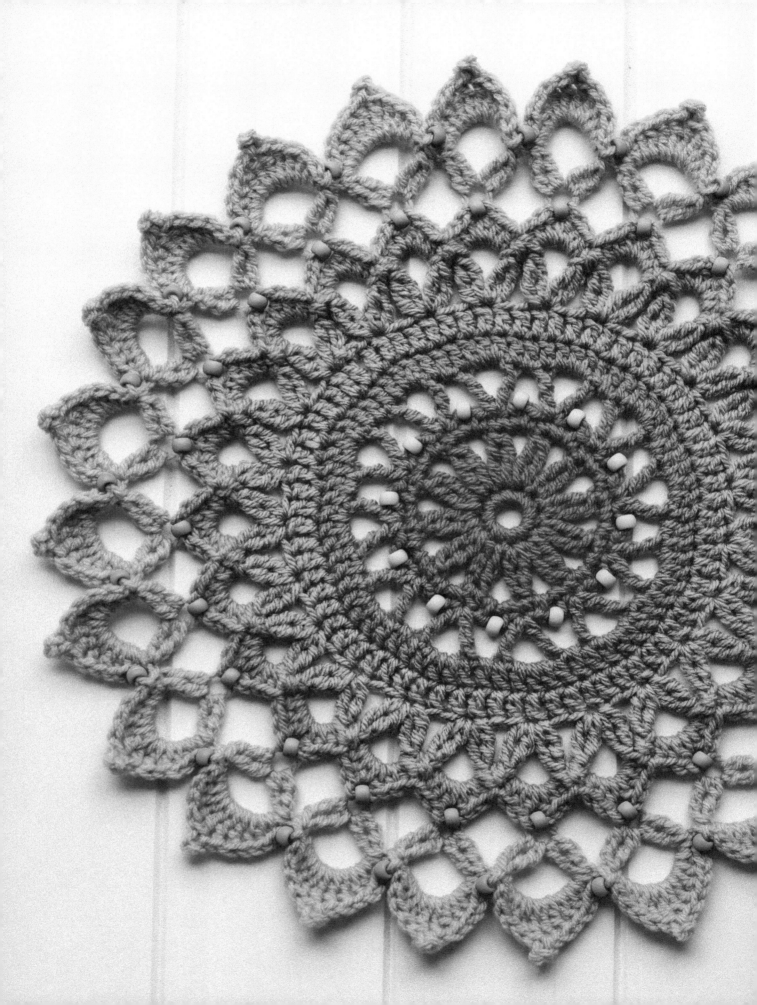

INSPIRE

MANDALA

verb. to fill with an animating, quickening, or exalting influence

Never interrupt a crocheter trying to find inspiration on Pinterest.

FINISHED SIZE

42cm/16.5in unblocked

MATERIALS

Special Aran
One ball of each

Colour 1 1320 Denim

Colour 2 1722 Storm Blue

Colour 3 1725 Sage

Colour 4 1712 Lime

Colour 5 1823 Mustard

US H/8 UK 6 (5mm) hook

Yarn Needle

Scissors

3mm Beads (see below)

NOTES & TIPS

Beads required

Round 3: 12 Beads

Round 8: 24 Beads

Round 10: 24 Beads

Feel free to complement (match) or contrast (opposite) the colours in your rounds with the beads.

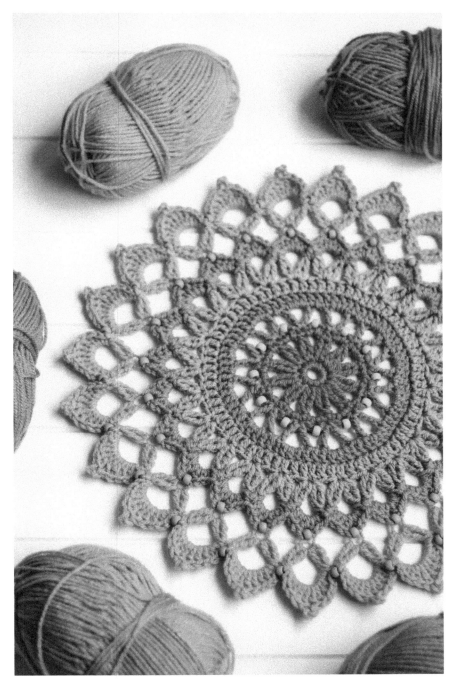

There is inspiration all around us.

Kapil Dev

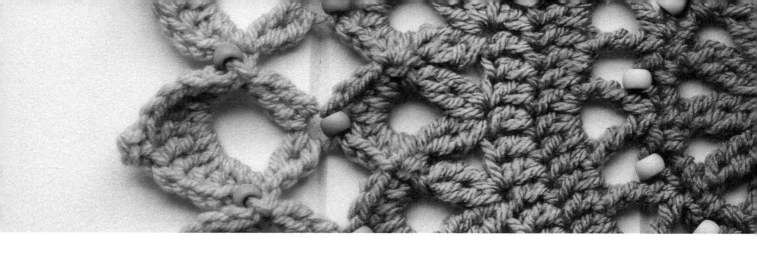

Round 1: C1

Make a MR, or (ch 8, join to first ch to form ring), ch 1 (doesn't count as st here and throughout), 12 sc in ring, join to first sc made, do not fasten off. *<12 sc>*

Round 2: C1

Beg tr2cl, ch 2, (tr2cl, ch 2) in each st around, join to first cl made, do not fasten off. *<12 tr2cl, 12 ch-2 sp>*

Round 3: C1

Ch 1, [sc in st, (sc, ch 1, IB, ch 1, sc) in ch-2 sp] around, join to first sc made, fasten off. *<36 sc, 12 beads, 24 ch-1 sp>*

Round 4: C2 – This round is worked in the middle sc between beads from Rnd 3 only

In middle sc between beads, make a standing [(tr, ch 3, tr) in middle sc, ch 1, sk st, sk bead, sk st] around, join to first tr made, do not fasten off. *<24 tr, 12 ch-3 sp, 12 ch-1 sp>*

Round 5: C2

Ch 3 (counts as dc), 3 dc in ch-3 sp, dc in next st, dc in ch-1 sp, place marker in this dc only, [dc in next st, 3 dc in ch-3 sp, dc in next st, dc in ch-1 sp] around, join to top of ch-3, fasten off. *<72 dc>*

Round 6: C3

In marked st, make a standing dc, dc in each st around, join to first dc made, do not fasten off. *<72 dc>*

Round 7: C3

Beg tr2cl, (ch 4, tr2cl) in same st, sk 2 sts, [(tr2cl, ch 4, tr2cl) in next st, sk 2 sts] around, join to first cl made, fasten off. *<48 tr2cl, 24 ch-4 sp>*

Round 8: C4

In any ch-4 sp, make a standing [(2 hdc, dc, ch 1, IB, ch 1, dc, 2 hdc) in ch-4 sp, fphdc2tog around next 2 cl] around, join to first hdc made, fasten off. *<96 hdc, 48 dc, 48 ch-1 sp, 24 beads, 24 fphdc2tog>*

Round 9: C5

In any loop behind any bead, make a standing [(tr2cl, ch 6, tr2cl) in each loop behind the bead] around, join to first cl made, do not fasten off. *<48 tr2cl, 24 ch-6 sp>*

Round 10: C5

In any ch-6 sp, make a standing [(sc, hdc, 2 dc, 2 tr, picot 3, 2 tr, 2 dc, hdc, sc) in ch-6 sp, IB, sk st, sl st in between cl, sk st] around, join to first sc made, fasten off. *<48 sc, 48 hdc, 96 dc, 96 tr, 24 picot 3, 24 beads, 24 sl st>*

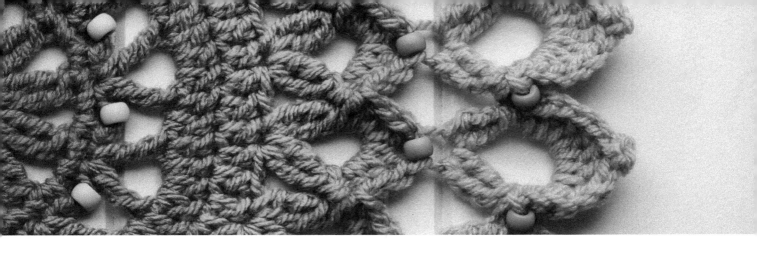

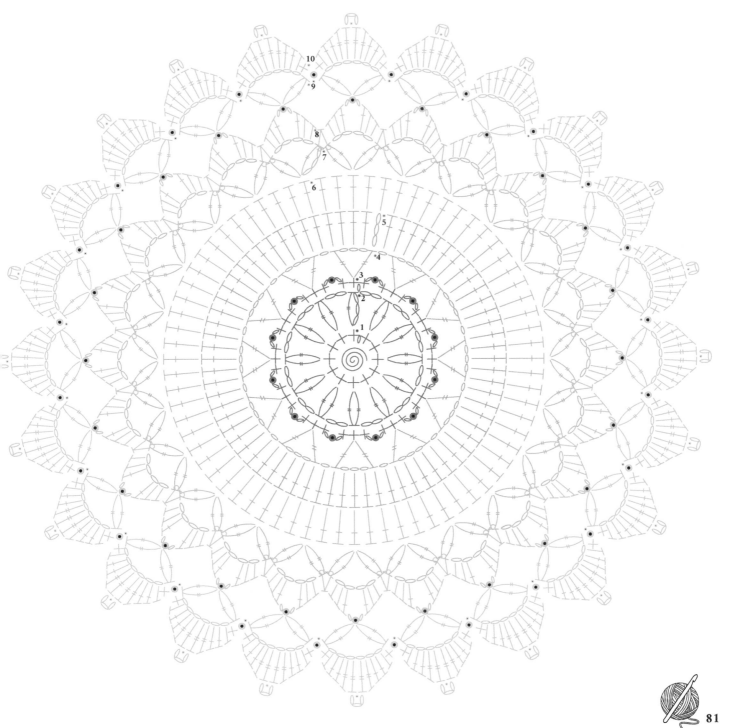

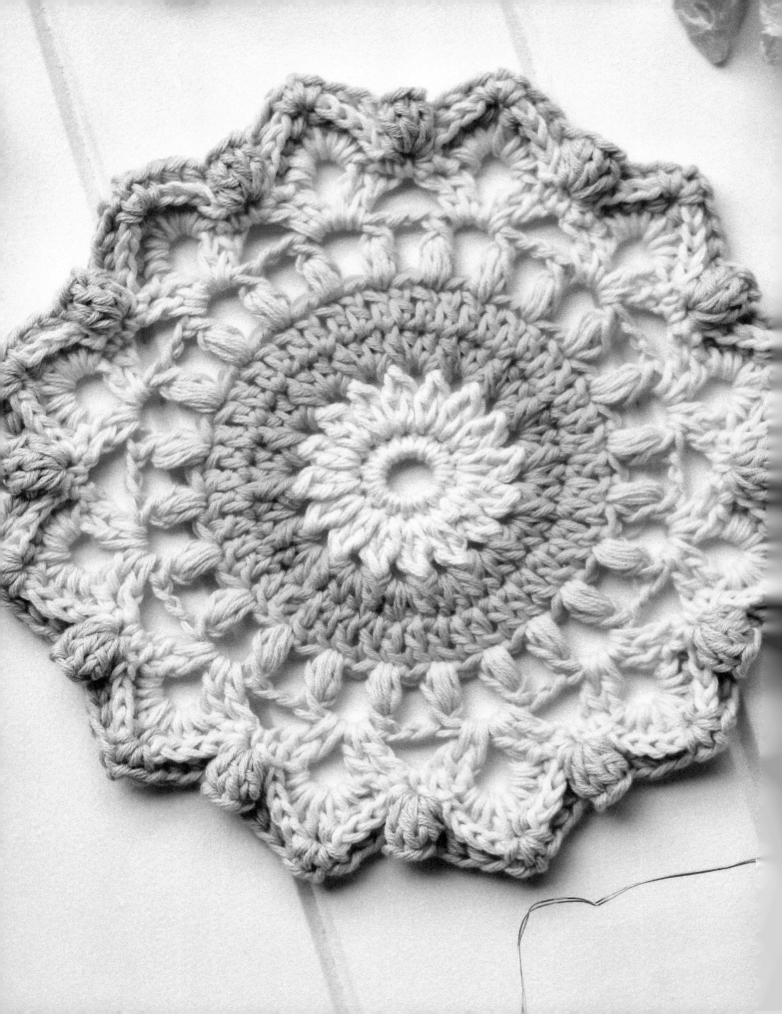

INTEGRITY

MANDALA

noun. adherence to moral and ethical principles; soundness of moral character; honesty

Integrity is your destiny, it is the light that guides your way - Plato

FINISHED SIZE

19cm/7.5in unblocked

MATERIALS

Naturals Organic Cotton
One ball of each

Colour 1 7183 Blossom

Colour 2 7178 Papaya

Colour 3 7180 Coral

Colour 4 7176 Peach

Colour 5 7174 Buttermilk

Colour 6 7193 Artichoke

US G/6 UK 8 (4mm) hook

Yarn Needle

Scissors

NOTES & TIPS

Project Idea

Join these motifs together to make a pretty table runner.

See next page for instructions.

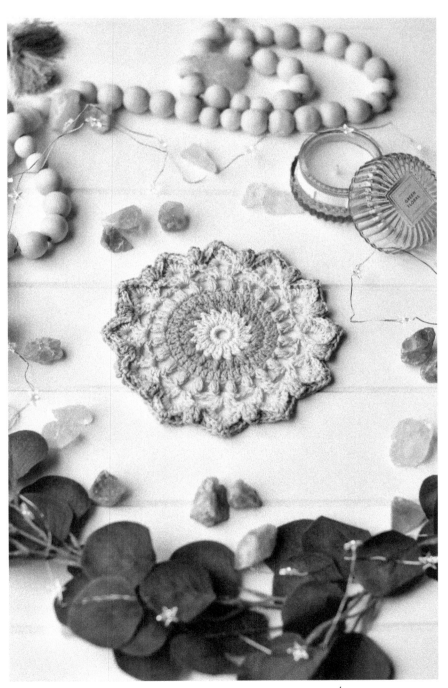

Integrity is doing the right thing, even when no one is watching.

C.S Lewis

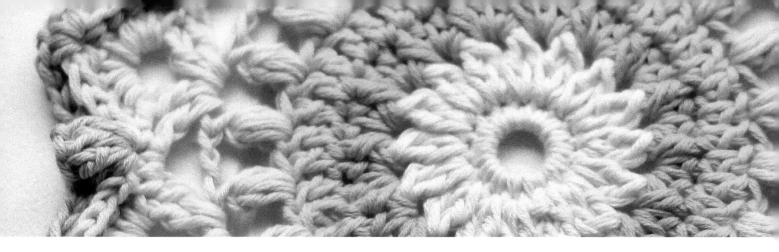

Round 1: C1

Make a MR, or (ch 9, join to first ch to form ring), ch 1 (doesn't count as st), 16 sc in ring, join to first sc made, do not fasten off. *<16 sc>*

Round 2: C1

Beg dc2cl, ch 2, (dc2cl, ch 2) in each st around, join to first cl made, fasten off. *<16 dc2cl, 16 ch-2 sp>*

Round 3: C2

Around any cl, make a standing [fphdc around cl, 2 hdc in ch-2 sp] around, join to first fphdc made, fasten off. *<16 fphdc, 32 hdc>*

Round 4: C3

Make a standing dc in each st around, join to first dc made, fasten off. *<48 dc>*

Round 5: C4

In dc made in fphdc, make a standing [puff 3, ch 2, sk st] around, join to first puff 3 made, fasten off. *<24 puff 3, 24 ch-2 sp>*

Round 6: C5

In any ch-2 sp, make a standing [(2 dc, ch 4, 2 dc) in ch-2 sp, ch 1, sk st, sk ch-2 sp, sk st] around, join to first dc made, do not fasten off. *<48 dc, 12 ch-4 sp, 12 ch-1 sp>*

Round 7: C5

Ch 1 (doesn't count as st), sc in same st as join, sk st, (4 dc, ch 2, 4 dc) in ch-4 sp, sk st, sc in next st, sc in ch-1 sp, [sc in next st, sk st, (4 dc, ch 2, 4 dc) in ch-4 sp, sk st, sc in next st, sc in ch-1 sp] around, join to first sc made, fasten off. *<96 dc, 36 sc, 12 ch-2 sp>*

Round 8: C6

In any ch-2 sp, make a standing [(sc, ch 2, sc) in ch-2 sp, bphdc around next 4 sts, ch 1, sk st, pop in next, ch 1, sk st, bphdc around next 4 sts] around, join to first sc made, fasten off. *<12 pop, 24 sc, 96 bphdc, 12 ch-2 sp>*

Joining Motifs:

Make one complete motif

On consecutive motifs, join in the ch-2 sp on round 8, but replace the ch-2 with a sc in the complete motif's ch-2 sp of round 8, then work round 8 back on the working motif.

Join in two points.

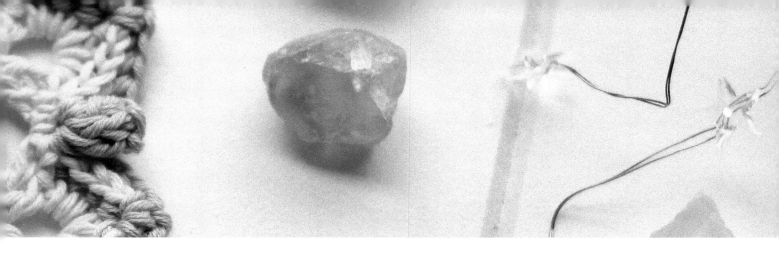

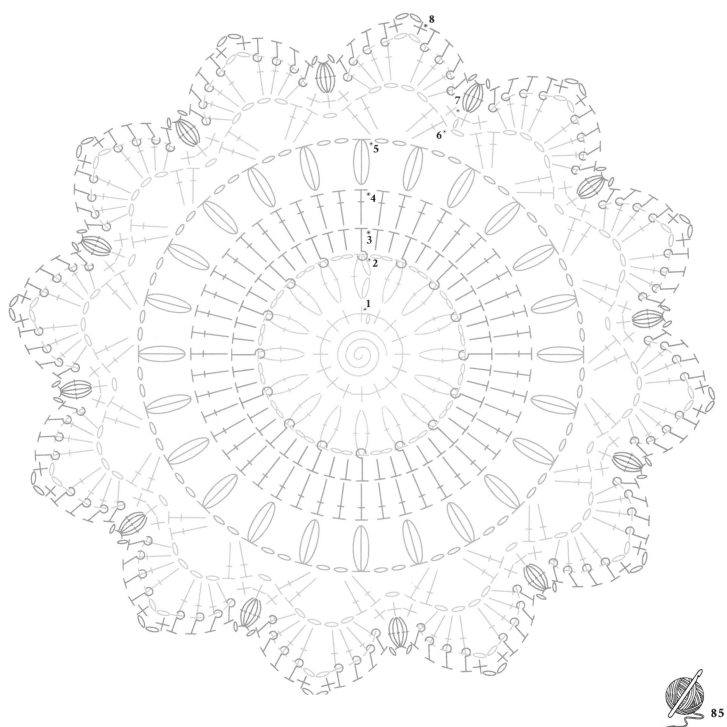

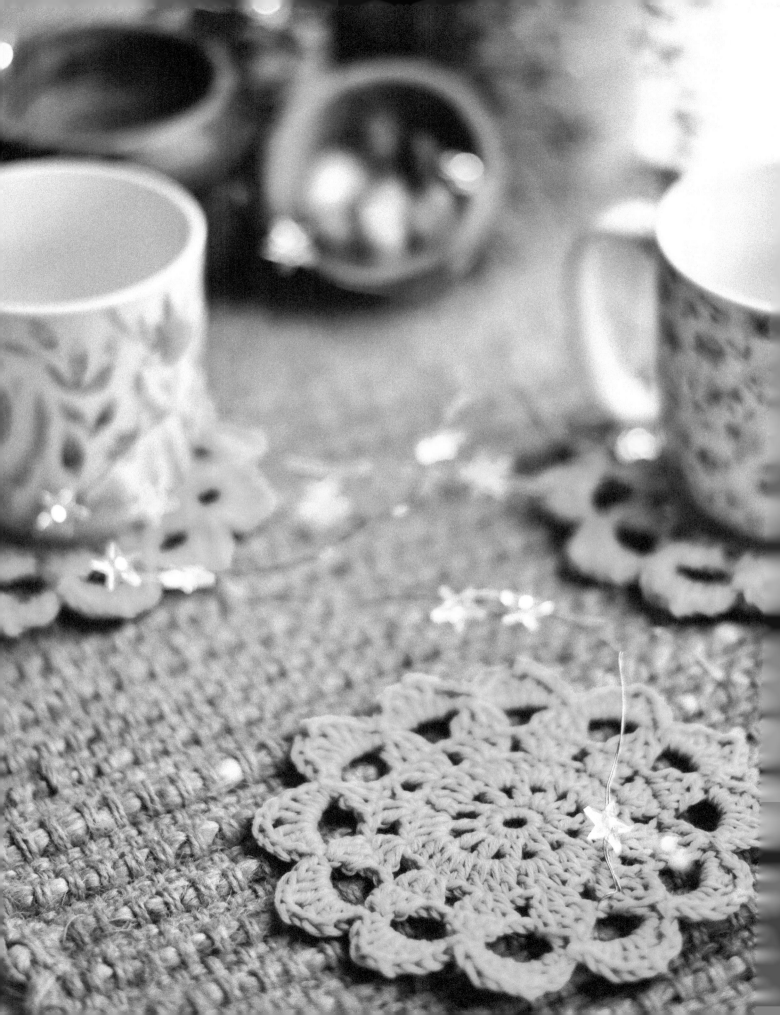

JOY

MANDALA

noun. the emotion of great delight or happiness caused by something exceptionally good or satisfying; keen pleasure; elation

What crocheters feel when they walk into a yarn store, buy yarn or meet a fellow crocheter.

FINISHED SIZE

14cm/5.5in unblocked

MATERIALS

Naturals Organic Cotton
One ball

Colour 1 7191 Jade

US G/6 UK 8 (4mm) hook
Yarn Needle
Scissors

NOTES & TIPS

Project Idea

Need a gift idea?
This motif works up nice and quick and sits lovely and flat, making it the ideal mandala for a coaster to gift.

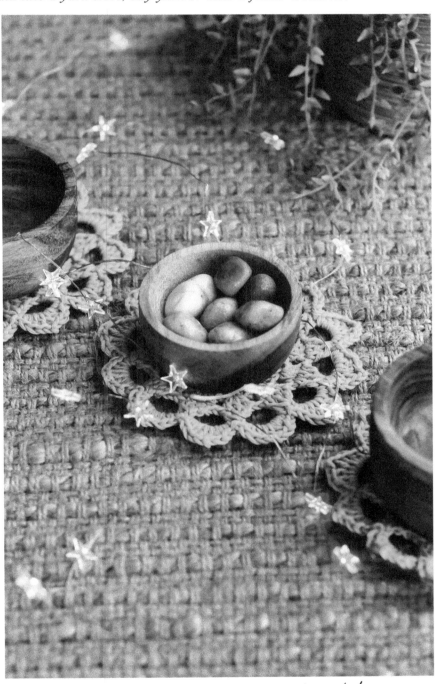

When the mind is pure, joy follows like a shadow that never leaves.

Buddha

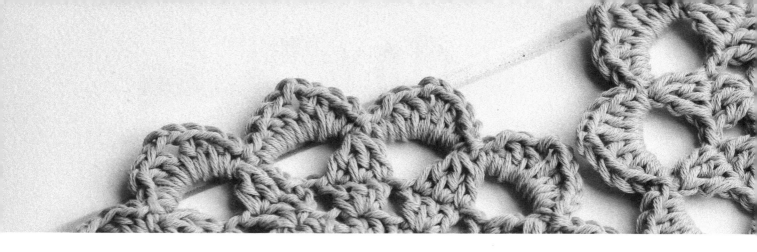

Round 1:

Make a MR, or (ch 6, join to first ch to form ring), ch 1 (doesn't count as st), 12 sc in ring, join to first sc made, do not fasten off. *<12 sc>*

Round 2:

Ch 4 (counts as dc + ch 1), (dc, ch 1) in each st around, join to 3rd ch of beg ch-4, do not fasten off. *<12 dc, 12 ch-1 sp>*

Round 3:

Sl st to ch-1 sp, ch 3 (counts as dc here and throughout), 2 dc in same sp, sk st, [3 dc in ch-1 sp, sk st] around, join to top of ch-3, do not fasten off. *<36 dc>*

Round 4:

Sl st to middle dc, ch 3, 2 dc in same st, ch 1, sk 2 sts, [3 dc in next st, ch 1, sk 2 sts] around, join to top of ch-3, do not fasten off. *<36 dc, 12 ch-1 sp>*

Round 5:

Beg dc3dec, ch 5, [dc3dec, ch 5, sk ch-1 sp] around, join to first dc3dec made, do not fasten off. *<12 dc3dec, 12 ch-5 sp>*

Round 6:

[(sc, hdc, 2 dc, ch 2, 2 dc, hdc, sc) in ch-5 sp, sl st in dc3dec] around, fasten off. *<24 sc, 24 hdc, 48 dc, 12 ch-2 sp, 12 sl st>*

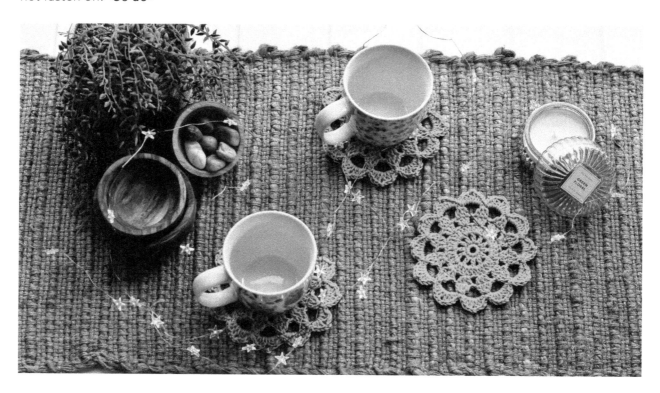

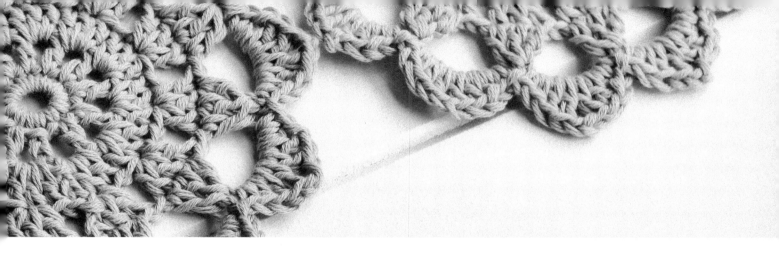

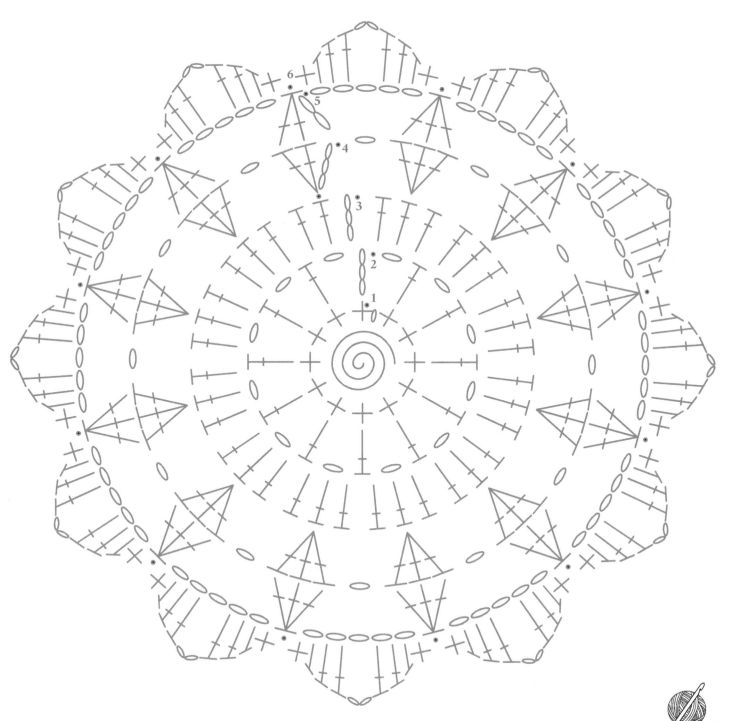

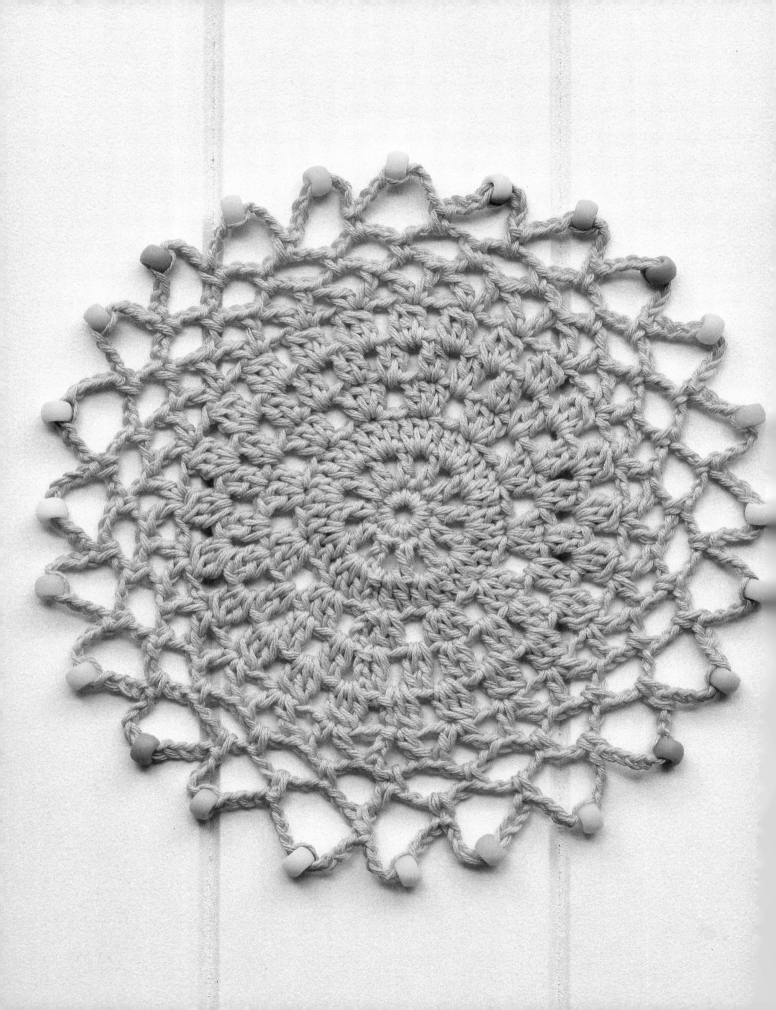

KINDNESS

MANDALA

noun. the state or quality of being kind

Showing kindness; weaving in your friend's ends without being asked.

FINISHED SIZE

21cm/8.2in unblocked

MATERIALS

Naturals Organic Cotton
One ball

Colour 1 7179 Flamingo

US G/6 UK 8 (4mm) hook
Small hook to insert beads
(anything from US B1 2.25 - UK 12
2.5mm)
Yarn Needle
Scissors
3mm Beads x 24

NOTES & TIPS

Project Idea

Jar or bowl cover
Have fun playing with colour and
maybe coloured beads like I have
done here :)

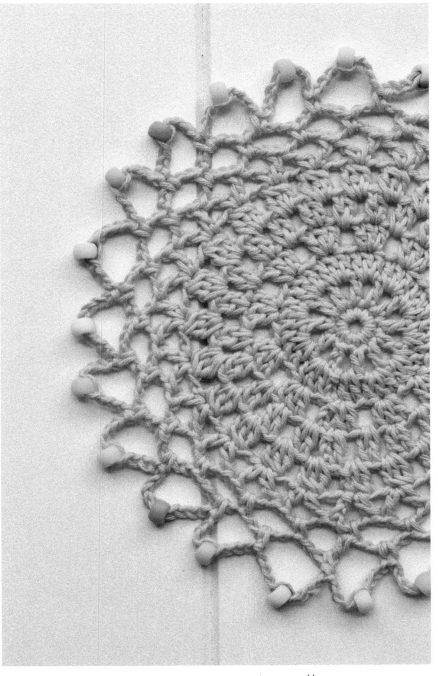

No act of kindness, no matter how small, is ever wasted

Aesop

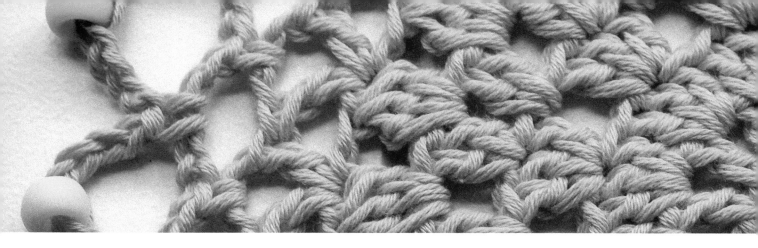

Round 1:

Make a MR, or (ch 6, join to first ch to form ring), ch 1 (doesn't count as st), 12 sc in ring, join to first sc made, do not fasten off. *<12 sc>*

Round 2:

Ch 4 (counts as dc + ch 1), (dc, ch 1) in each st around, join to third ch of beg ch-4, do not fasten off. *<12 dc, 12 ch-1 sp>*

Round 3:

Sl st to ch-1 sp, ch 3 (counts as dc here and throughout), 2 dc in same sp, sk st, [3 dc in ch-1 sp, sk st] around, join to top of ch-3, do not fasten off. *<36 dc>*

Round 4:

Sl st to middle dc, ch 3, 2 dc in same st, ch 1, sk 2 sts, [3 dc in next st, ch 1, sk 2 sts] around, join to top of ch-3, do not fasten off. *<36 dc, 12 ch-1 sp>*

Round 5:

Sl st to middle dc, ch 3, dc in same st, ch 1, sk st, 2 dc in ch-1 sp, ch 1, sk st, [2 dc in next st, ch 1, sk st, 2 dc in ch-1 sp, ch 1, sk st] around, join to top of ch-3, do not fasten off. *<48 dc, 24 ch-1 sp>*

Round 6:

Sl st to ch-1 sp, beg dc3cl, ch 2, sk 2 sts, [dc-3cl in ch-1 sp, ch 2, sk 2 sts] around, join to first cl made, do not fasten off. **<24 dc3cl, 24 ch-2 sp>**

Round 7:

Ch 6 (counts as dc + ch 3), dc in same st, sk 2 ch-sp, (dc, ch 3, dc) in each cl around, join to third ch of beg ch-6, do not fasten off. *<48 dc, 24 ch-3 sp>*

Round 8:

Sl st in first ch of ch-3 sp, sc in ch-3 sp, ch 5, [sc in ch-3 sp, ch 5] around, on last repeat, ch 2, dc into first sc made (this replaces the sl st join and places you at the correct starting point for the next round), do not fasten off. *<24 sc, 24 ch-5 sp>*

Round 9:

Sc in last ch-sp (same as dc join), ch 4, IB, ch 4, sk st, [sc in ch-5 sp, ch 4, IB, ch 4] around, join to first sc, fasten off. *<24 sc, 24 IB, 48 ch-4 sp>*

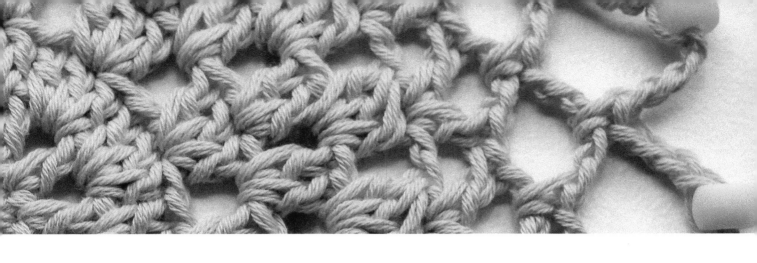

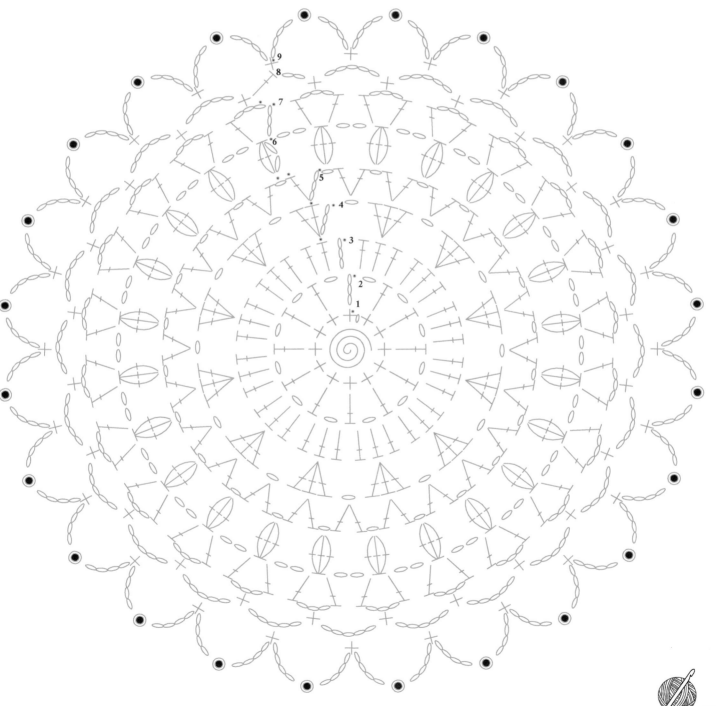

9
8
7
6
5
4
3
2
1

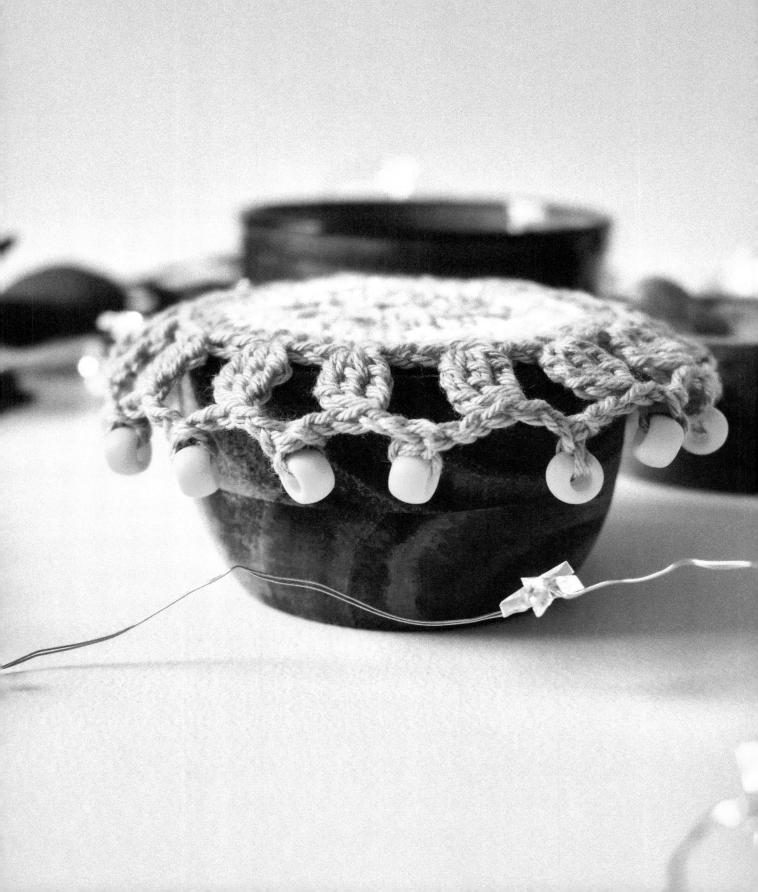

LOYALTY

MANDALA

noun. the state or quality of being loyal; faithfulness to commitments or obligations

Some crocheters find it a little bit hard to stay loyal to one WIP, that's completely okay.

FINISHED SIZE

13cm/5.11in unblocked

MATERIALS

Naturals Bamboo & Cotton
One ball of each

Colour 1 7128 Ecru

Colour 2 7143 Seafoam

Colour 3 7142 Sky

Colour 4 7140 Cornflower

US E/4; UK 9; (3.5mm) hook

Yarn Needle

Scissors

3mm Beads x 16

NOTES & TIPS

Project Idea

This makes the perfect coaster or wine or glass cover.

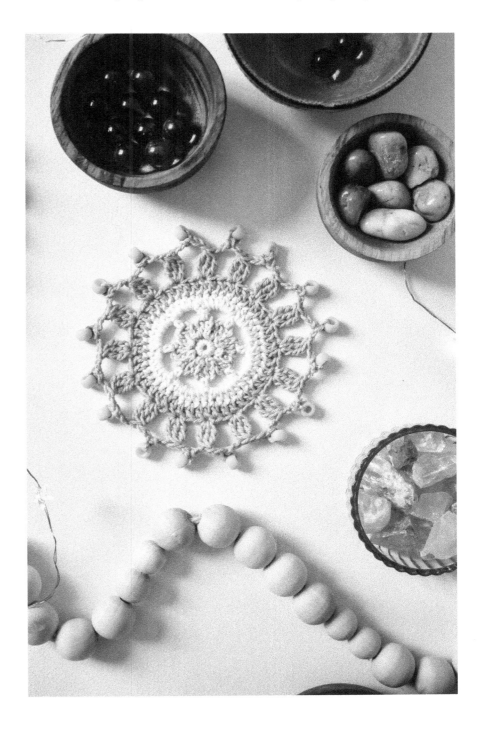

Loyalty is rare. If you find it, keep it.

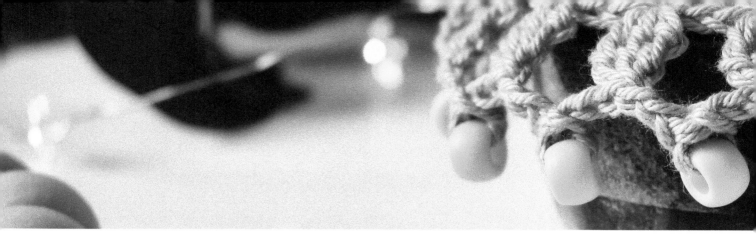

Round 1: C1

Make a MR, or (ch 4, join to first ch to form ring), ch 1 (doesn't count as st), 8 sc in ring, join to first sc made. *<8 sc>*

Round 2: C2

(sl st, ch 3, dc, ch 3, sl st) in each st around, fasten off. *<16 sl st, 16 ch-3 sp, 8 dc>*

Round 3: C1

Make a standing [hdc in dc, ch 3] around, join to first hdc made, do not fasten off. *<8 hdc, 8 ch-3 sp>*

Round 4: C1

Sl st to ch-3 sp, ch 2 (counts as hdc), 5 hdc in ch-3 sp, [sk st, 6 hdc in ch-3 sp] around, join to top of ch-2, fasten off. *<48 hdc>*

Round 5: C3

Make a standing dc in first hdc made in prev rnd, dc in each st around, join to first dc made, fasten off. *<48 dc>*

Round 6: C4

In first dc made in prev rnd, make a standing [tr3cl in dc, ch 4, IB, ch 1, sl st in 3rd ch under bead just made, ch 2, sk 2 sts] around, join to first cl made, fasten off. *<16 tr3cl, 16 Beads>*

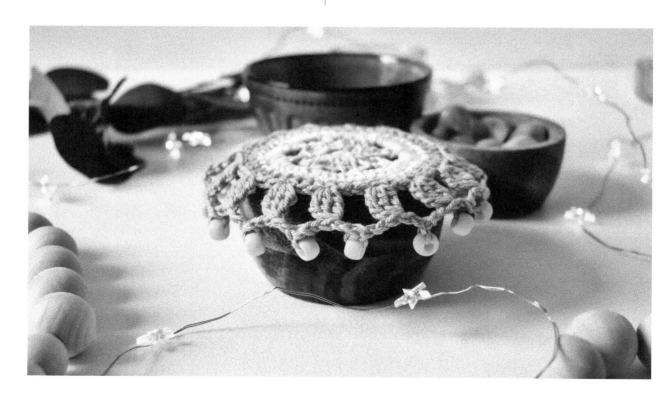

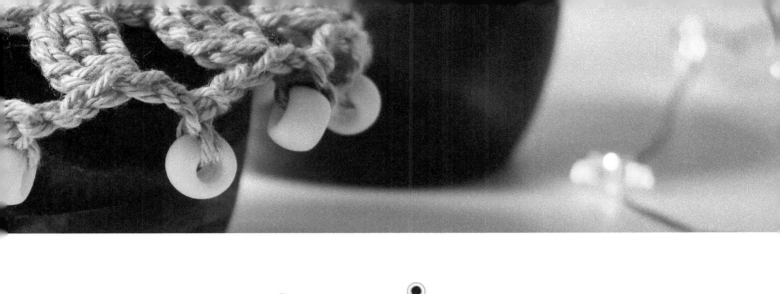

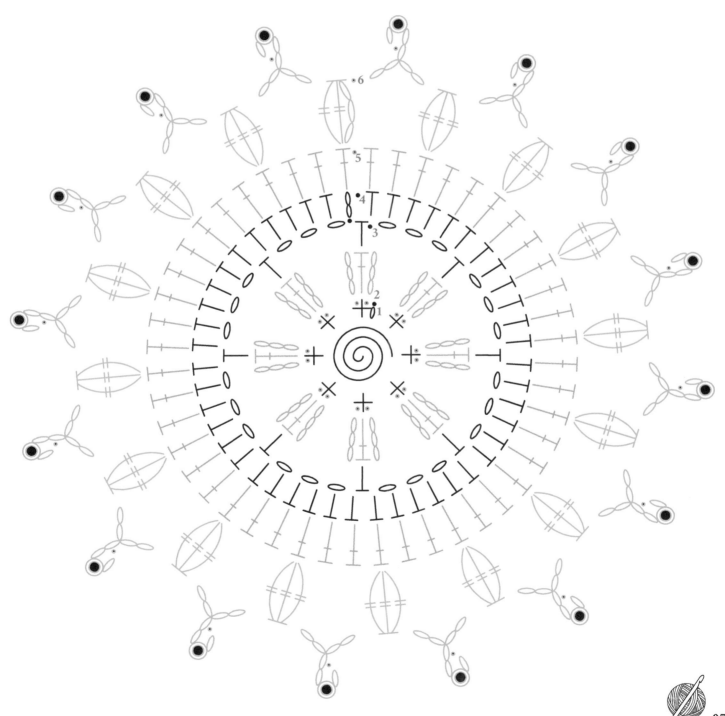

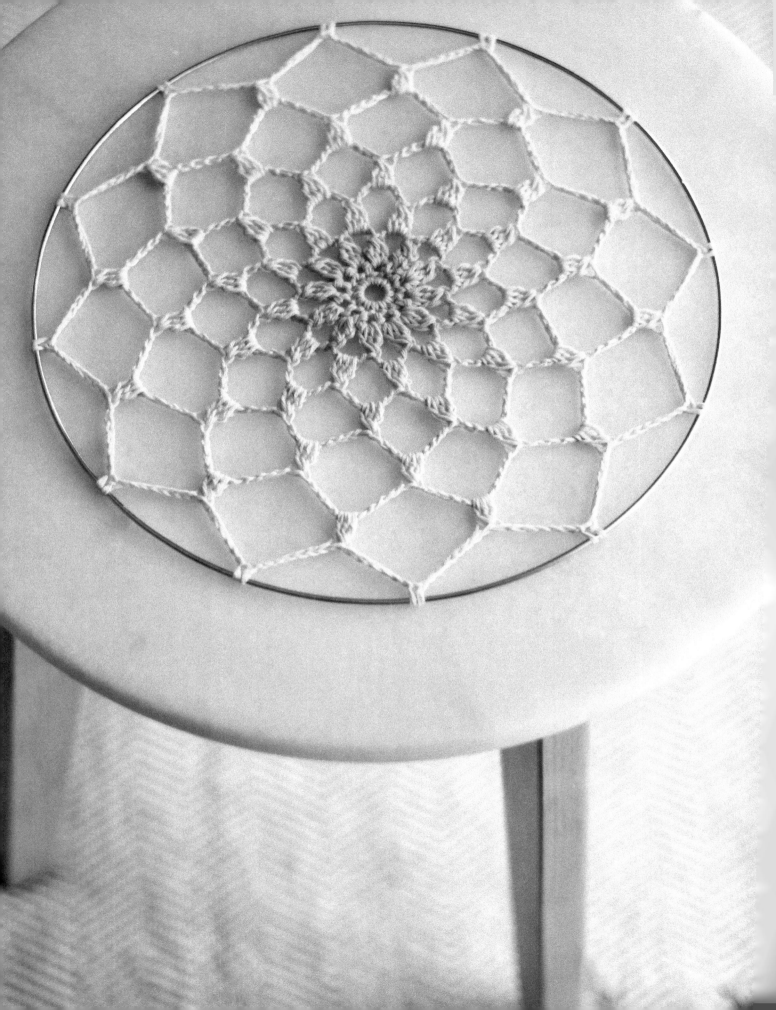

MINDFULNESS
M A N D A L A

noun. the state or quality of being mindful or aware of something

Be present in the moment of each stitch, pay attention to every movement you make.

FINISHED SIZE

30cm/7.5in attached to ring

MATERIALS

Naturals Organic Cotton
One ball of each

Colour 1 7169 Fondant

Colour 2 7177 Blush

Colour 3 7176 Peach

Colour 4 7174 Buttermilk

Colour 5 7172 Peppermint

US G/6 UK 8 (4mm) hook

Yarn Needle

Scissors

30cm ring pictured here

NOTES & TIPS

Attach to Ring

Make sure the ring is at least 5-10cm larger than your finished piece as the open-work of this mandala makes it really stretchy.

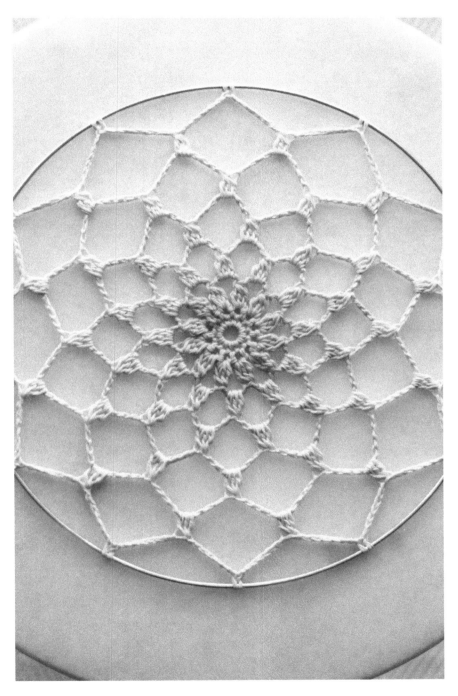

Mindfulness is being present without judgement in every moment.

Round 1: C1

Make a MR, or (ch 6, join to first ch to form ring), ch 1 (doesn't count as st), 12 sc in ring, join to first sc made, do not fasten off. *<12 sc>*

Round 2: C1

[Ch 3, sl st in next st] around, do not fasten off. *<12 ch-3 sp, 12 sl st>*

Round 3: C1

Sl st to ch-3 sp, beg dc3cl in same sp, ch 4, sk sl st, [dc3cl in ch-3 sp, ch 4, sk sl st] around, join to first cl made, fasten off. *<12 dc3cl, 12 ch-4 sp>*

Round 4: C2

Make a standing [(dc3cl, ch 6) in ch-4 sp, sk st] around, join to first cl made, fasten off.

<12 dc3cl, 12 ch-6 sp>

Round 5: C3

Make a standing [(dc3cl, ch 8) in ch-6 sp, sk st] around, join to first cl made, fasten off.

<12 dc3cl, 12 ch-8 sp>

Round 6: C4

Make a standing [(dc3cl, ch 10) in ch-8 sp, sk st] around, join to first cl made, fasten off.

<12 dc3cl, 12 ch-10 sp>

Round 7: Using C5

Make a standing [dc3cl in ch-8 sp, ch 7, sc onto ring, ch 7, sk st] around, join to first cl made, fasten off.

<12 dc3cl, 12 sc, 24 ch-7 sp>

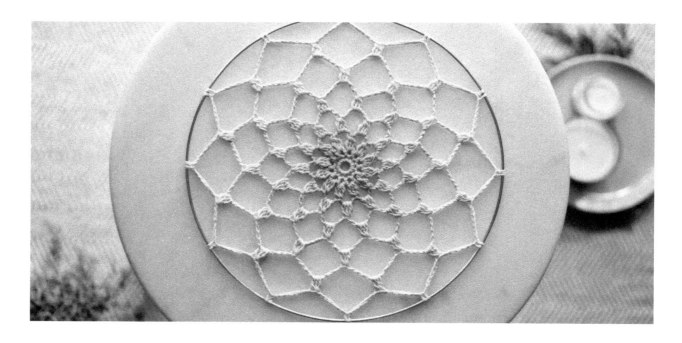

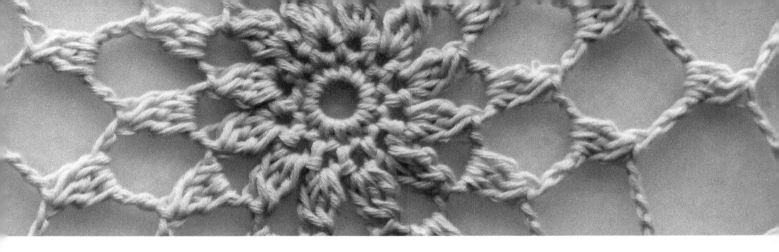

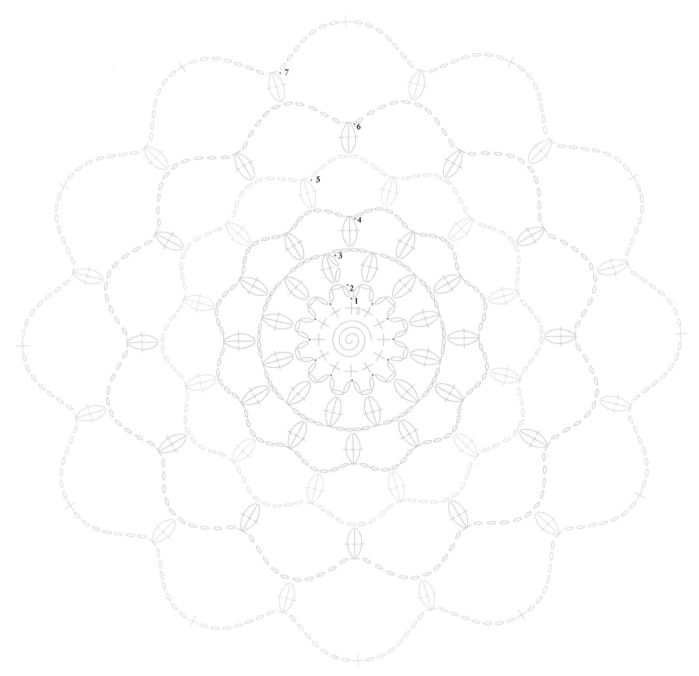

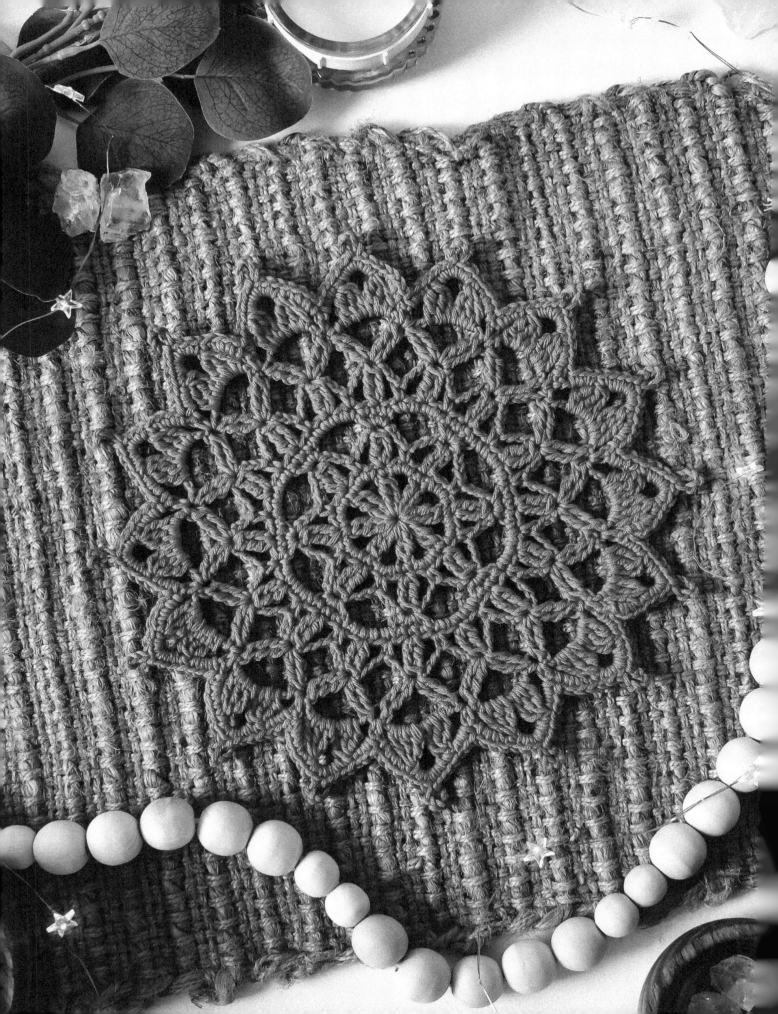

OPTIMISM
MANDALA

noun. a disposition or tendency to look on the more favorable side of events or conditions and to expect the most favorable outcome

'Just one more round', said the crocheter with great optimism.

FINISHED SIZE

25cm/9.8in unblocked

MATERIALS

Naturals Organic Cotton
One ball

Colour 1 7200 Blue Dusk

US G/6 UK 8 (4mm) hook
Yarn Needle
Scissors

NOTES & TIPS

Project Idea

Jar or bowl cover
Have fun playing with colour and if you are feeling adventurous, you could add beads or turn it into a bowl.

Do not fasten off after each round unless you are playing around with different colours.

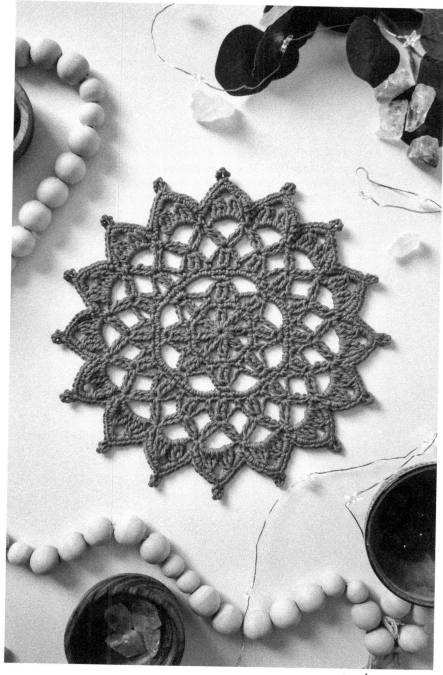

Part of being optimistic is keeping one's head pointed toward the sun, one's feet moving forward.

Nelson Mandela

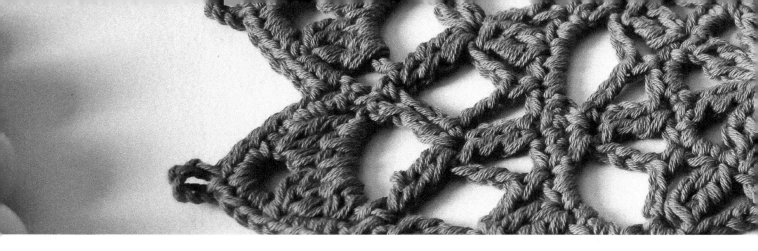

Round 1:

Make a MR, or (ch 4, join to first ch to form ring), beg tr2cl, ch 3, (tr2cl, ch 3) 7 times in ring, join to top of beg tr2cl, do not fasten off. *<8 tr2cl, 8 ch-3 sp>*

Round 2:

Ch 1 (doesn't count as st here and through-out), sc in same st as join, 3 sc in ch-3 sp, [sc in next st, 3 sc in ch-3 sp] around, join to first sc made, do not fasten off. *<32 sc>*

Round 3:

Beg tr2cl in same st as join, ch 3, sk st, sc in next st, ch 3, sk st, [tr2cl in next st, ch 3, sk st, sc in next st, ch 3, sk st] around, join to first cl made, do not fasten off.

<8 tr2cl, 8 sc, 16 ch-3 sp>

Round 4: *This round is worked only in tr2cl sts from previous round*

Ch 1, [3 sc in same tr2cl st, ch 5] around, join to first sc made, do not fasten off.

<24 sc, 8 ch-5 sp>

Round 5:

Ch 1, sc in same st as join, sc in next 2 sts, 5 sc in ch-5 sp, [sc in next 3 sts, 5 sc in ch-5 sp] around, join to first sc made, do not fasten off. *<64 sc>*

Round 6:

Sl st to next sc, beg tr2cl in same st as join, ch 3, sk st, sc in next, ch 3, sk st, [tr2cl in next, ch 3, sk st, sc in next, ch 3, sk st] around, join to first cl made, do not fasten off. *<16 tr2cl, 16 sc, 32 ch-3 sp>*

Round 7: *This round is worked only in tr2cl sts from previous round*

(Beg tr2cl, ch 7, tr2cl) in same st, (tr2cl, ch 7, tr2cl) in each st around, join to first cl made, do not fasten off. *<32 tr2cl, 16 ch-7 sp>*

Round 8:

Ch 1, sc in same st as join, (ch 3, tr3cl, ch 3, tr3cl) in ch-7 sp, ch 3, sk tr2cl, [sc in next tr2cl, (ch 3, tr3cl, ch 3, tr3cl) in ch-7 sp, ch 3, sk tr2cl] around, join to first sc made, do not fasten off. *<32 sc, 32 tr3cl, 48 ch-3 sp >*

Round 9:

Ch 1, starting in first first ch-3 sp made, [3 sc in ch-3 sp, sc in st, (3 sc, picot 5, 3 sc) in ch-3 sp, sc in st, 3 sc in ch-3 sp, sk st] around, join to first sc made, fasten off.

<224 sc, 16 picot 5>

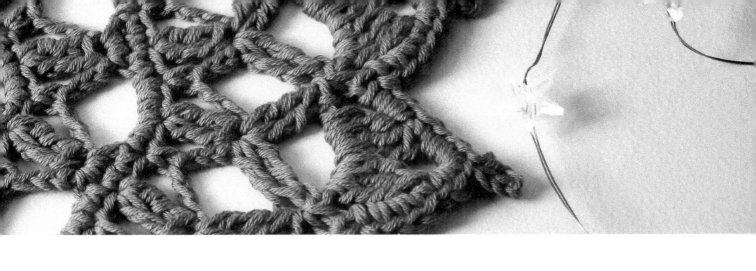

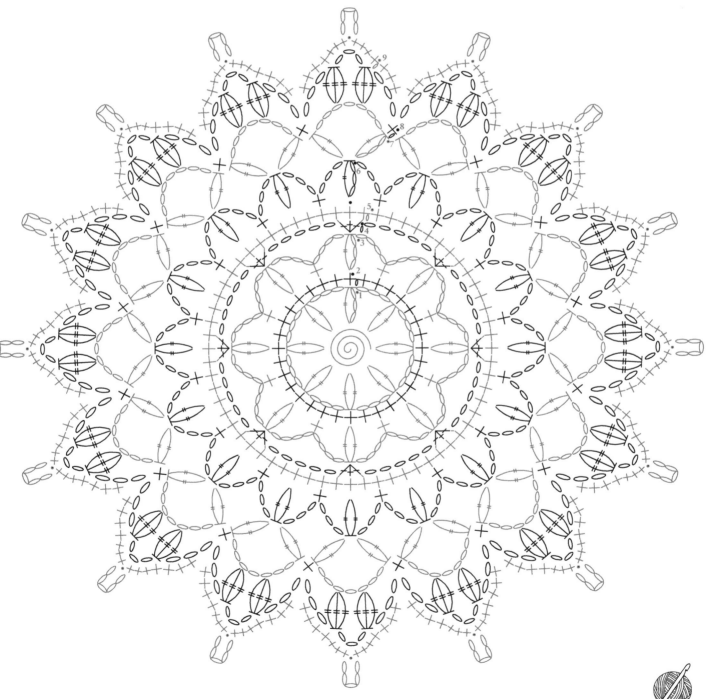

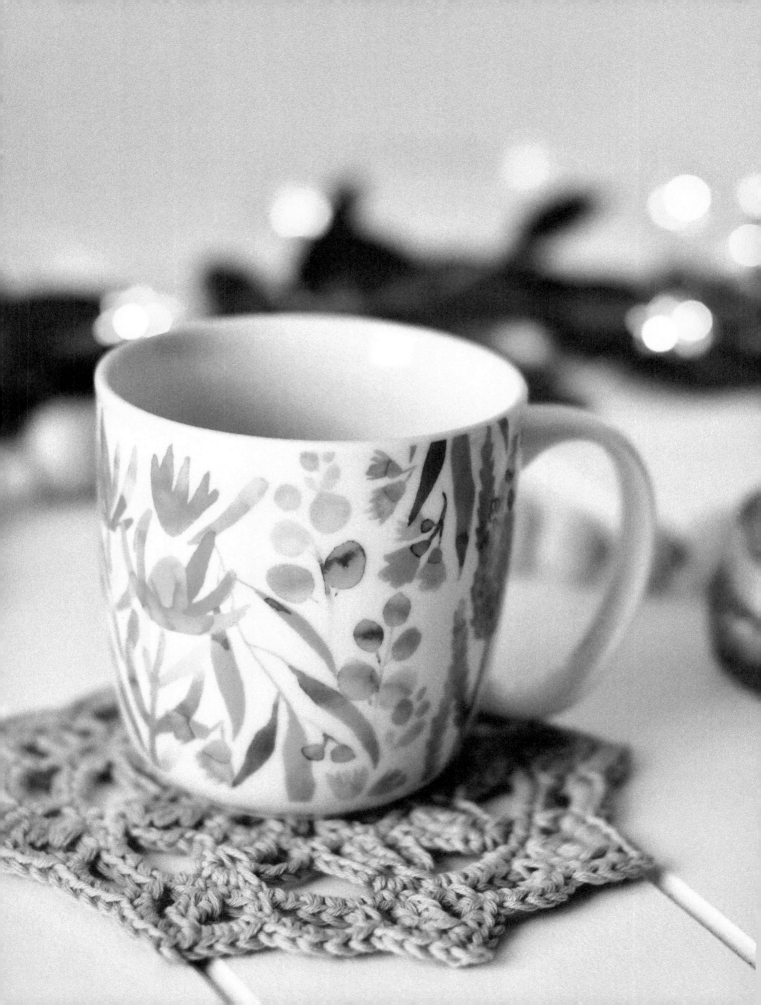

ORIGINALITY

MANDALA

noun. ability to think or express oneself in an independent and individual manner; creative ability

As long as you like or love your project, that's all that matters. It's yours. Original. You.

FINISHED SIZE

25cm/9.8in unblocked

MATERIALS

Naturals Organic Cotton
One ball

Colour 1 7196 Sage

US G/6 UK 8 (4mm) hook

Yarn Needle

Scissors

NOTES & TIPS

Project Idea

Coaster or small wall hanging

Do not fasten off after each round unless you are playing around with different colours.

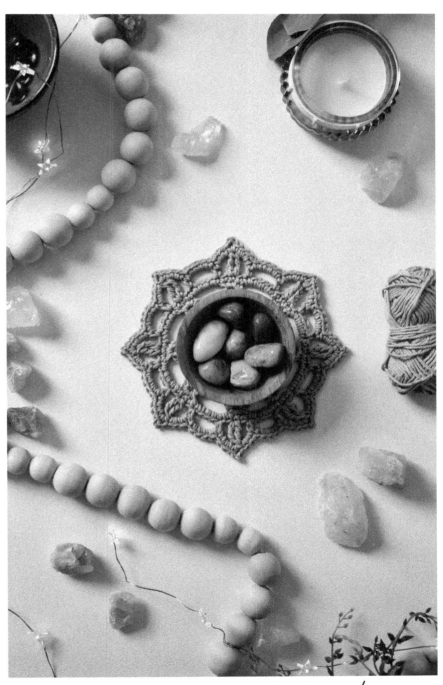

It is better to fail in originality than to succeed in imitation.

Herman Melville

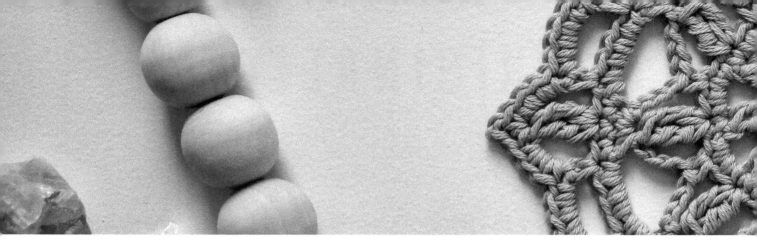

Round 1:
Make a MR, or (ch 4, join to first ch to form ring), beg tr2cl, ch 3, (tr2cl, ch 3) 7 times, join to top of beg tr2cl, do not fasten off. *<8 tr2cl, 8 ch-3 sp>*

Round 2:
Ch 1 (doesn't count as st here and through-out), sc in same st as join, 3 sc in ch-3 sp, [sc in next st, 3 sc in ch-3 sp] around, join to first sc made, do not fasten off. *<32 sc>*

Round 3:
Beg tr2cl in same st as join, ch 4, sk st, sc in next st, ch 4, sk st, [tr2cl in next st, ch 4, sk st, sc in next st, ch 4, sk st] around, join to first tr2cl made, do not fasten off.
<8 tr2cl, 8 sc, 16 ch-4 sp>

Round 4: *This round is worked only in tr2cl sts from previous round.*
Ch 1, 3 sc in same tr2cl st, ch 5, [3 sc in next cl, ch 5] around, join to first sc made, do not fasten off. *<24 sc, 8 ch-5 sp>*

Round 5:
Ch 1, sc in same st as join, sc in next 2 sts, 5 sc in ch-5 sp, [sc in next 3 sts, 5 sc in ch-5 sp] around, join to first sc made, do not fasten off. *<64 sc>*

Round 6:
Sl st to next st, beg tr2cl, ch 3, sk st, sc in next, ch 5, sk 3 sts, sc in next, ch 3, sk st, [tr-2cl in next st, ch 3, sk st, sc in next st, ch 5, sk 3 sts, sc in next st, ch 3, sk st] around, join to first tr2cl made, do not fasten off. *<8 tr2cl, 16 sc, 8 ch-5 sp, 16 ch-3 sp>*

Round 7:
Ch 1, [(sc, ch 2, sc) in tr2cl st, 3 sc in ch-3 sp, sk st, 5 sc in ch-5 sp, sk st, 3 sc in ch-3 sp] around, join to first sc made, fasten off, do not fasten off. *<104 sc, 8 ch-2 sp>*

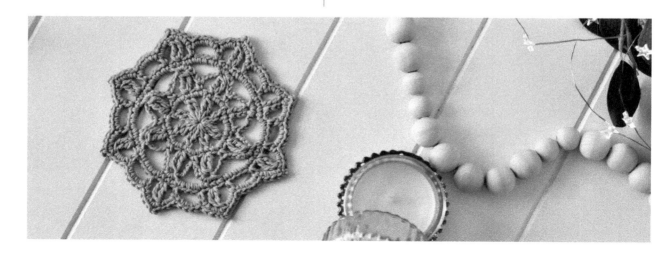

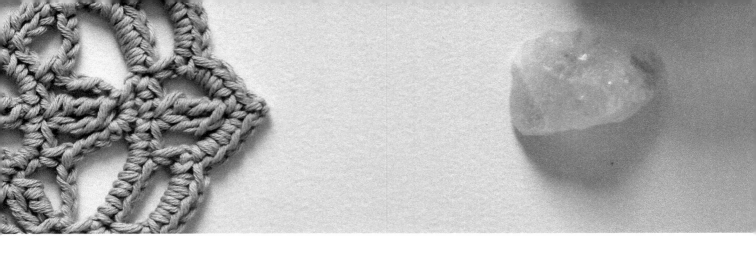

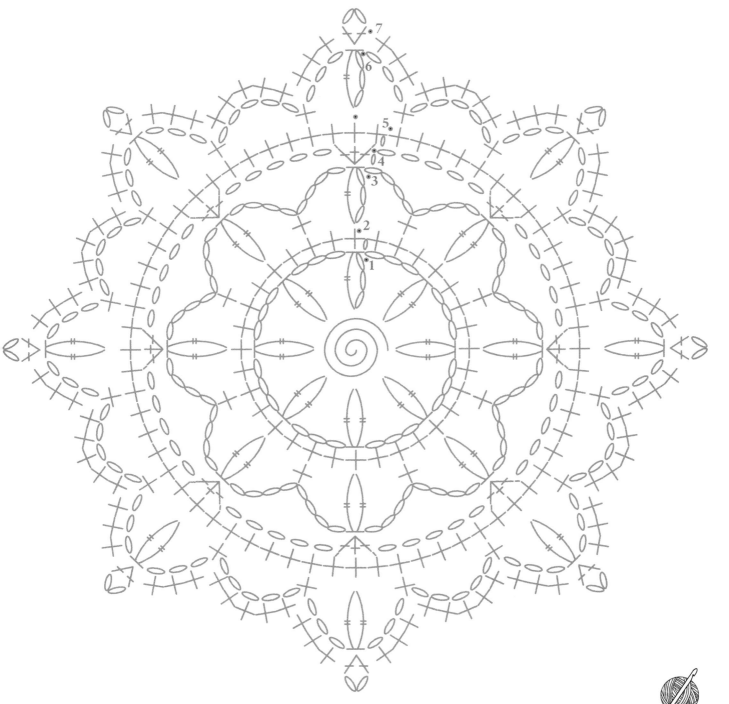

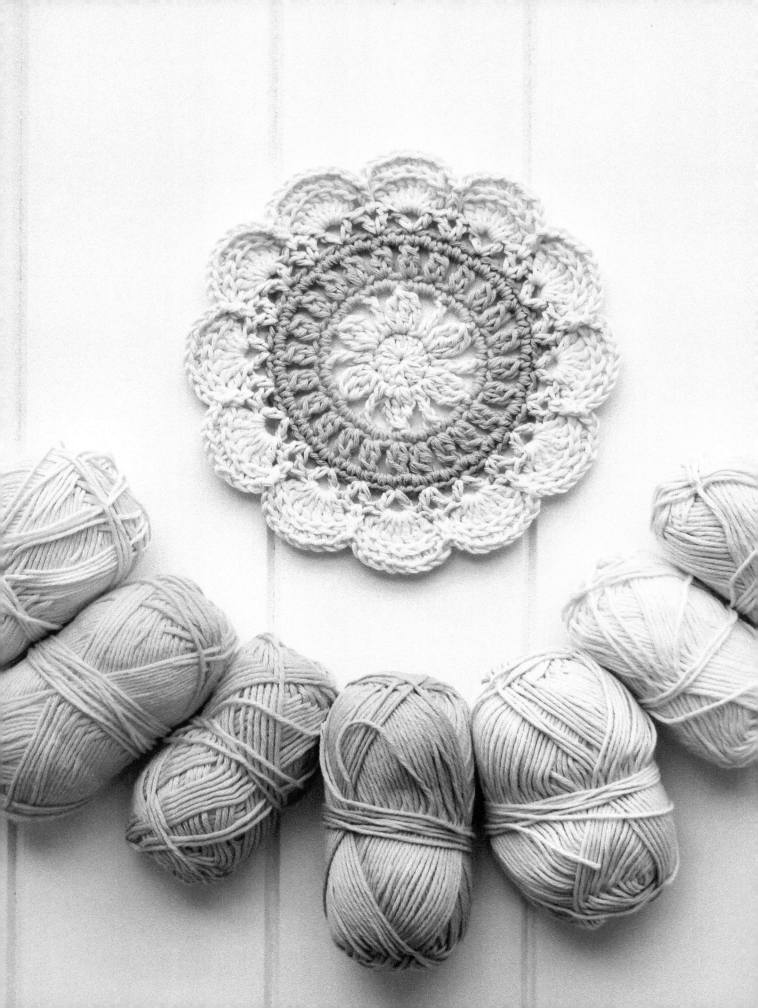

PATIENCE

M A N D A L A

noun. quiet, steady perseverance; even-tempered care; diligence
Crocheters are filled with patience. Because they don't want to frog, ever.

FINISHED SIZE

17cm/6.7in unblocked

MATERIALS

Naturals Organic Cotton
One ball of each

Colour 1 7174 Buttermilk
Colour 2 7180 Coral
Colour 3 7169 Fondant
Colour 4 7184 Mauve
Colour 5 7195 Faded Denim
Colour 6 7197 Blue Lagoon
Colour 7 7172 Peppermint

US G-6 / UK 8 / (4mm) hook
Yarn Needle
Scissors

NOTES & TIPS

Round 8
Pay attention to where the hdc stitches are placed. Don't make a boo-boo and forget to skip the sc stitches.

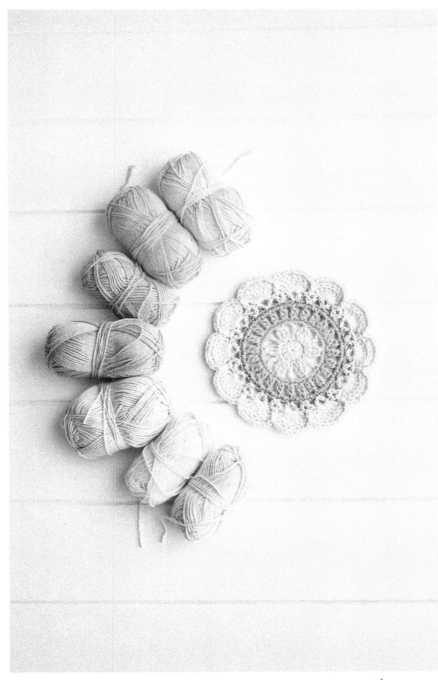

Have patience with all things, but first of all with yourself.

Saint Francis de Sales

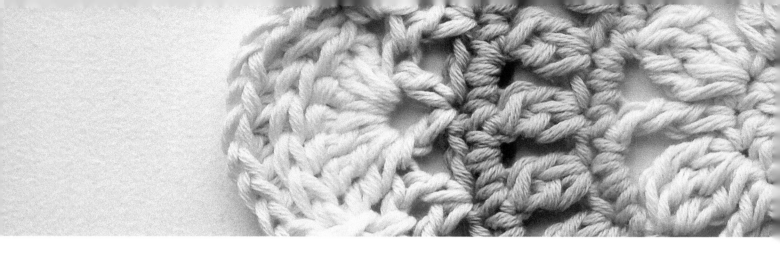

Round 1: C1

Make a MR, or (ch 4, join to first ch to form ring), ch 3 counts as dc, 11 dc in ring, join to top of ch-3, do not fasten off. <12 dc>

Round 2: C1

Sl st to next st, beg tr3cl, ch 2, tr in next st, ch 2, [tr3cl in next st, ch 2, tr in next st, ch 2] around, join to first cl made, fasten off. *<6 tr3cl, 6 tr, 12 ch-2 sp>*

Round 3: C2

In any cl, make a standing [sc in tr3cl, 3 sc in ch-2 sp, sc in tr, 3 sc in ch-2 sp] around, join to first sc made, fasten off. *<48 sc>*

Round 4: C3

In any sc in cl, make a standing [dc2cl, ch 2, sk st] around, join to first cl made, fasten off. *<24 dc2cl, 24 ch-2 sp>*

Round: 5 C2

In first cl made in prev rnd, make a standing [sc in st, 2 sc in ch-2 sp] around, join to first sc made, fasten off. *<72 sc>*

Round 6: C1

In first st made in prev rnd, make a standing [(dc, ch 2, dc) in st, sk 2 sts] around, join to first dc made, fasten off. *<24 v st>*

Round 7: C3:

In first ch-2 sp made, make a standing [7 tr in v st, sk 2 sts, sc in next v st, sk 2 sts] around, join to first tr made, fasten off. *<84 tr, 12 sc>*

Round 8: C2 - *Work hdc sts only in 3rd loop*

Make a standing [fpsc around sc, (hdc in next st, 2 hdc in next st) three times, hdc in next st] around, join to first fpsc made. Fasten off. *<12 fpsc, 120 hdc in 3rd loop>*

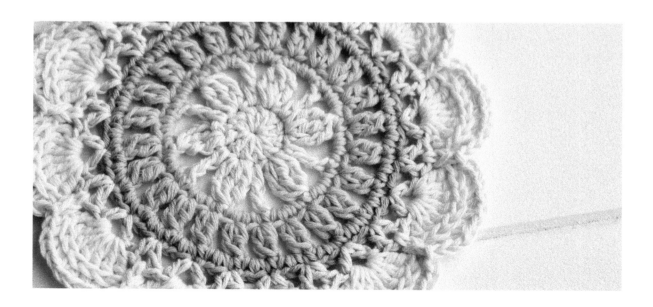

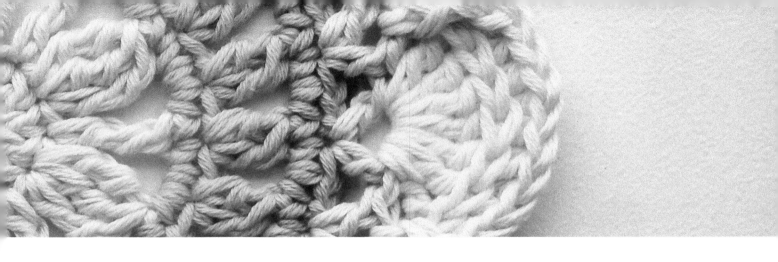

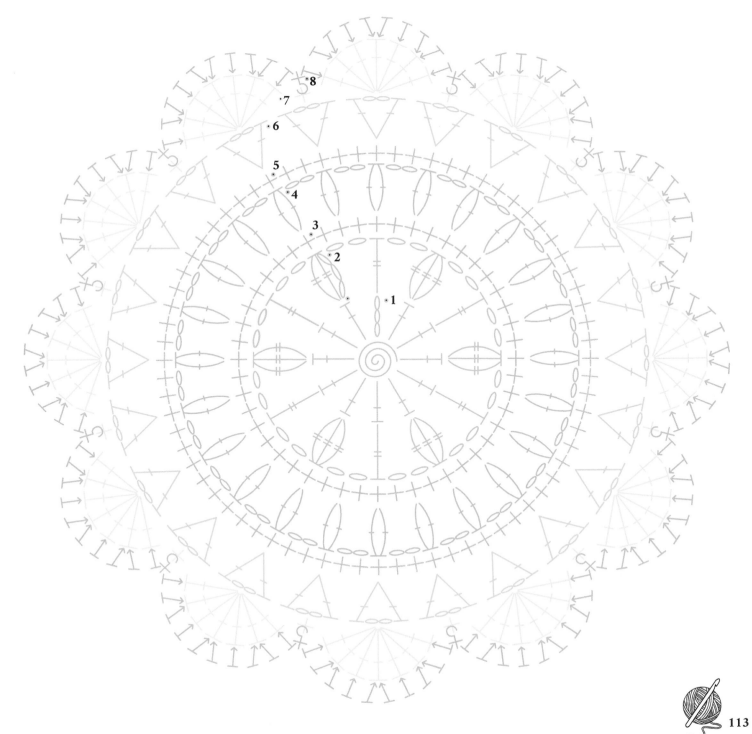

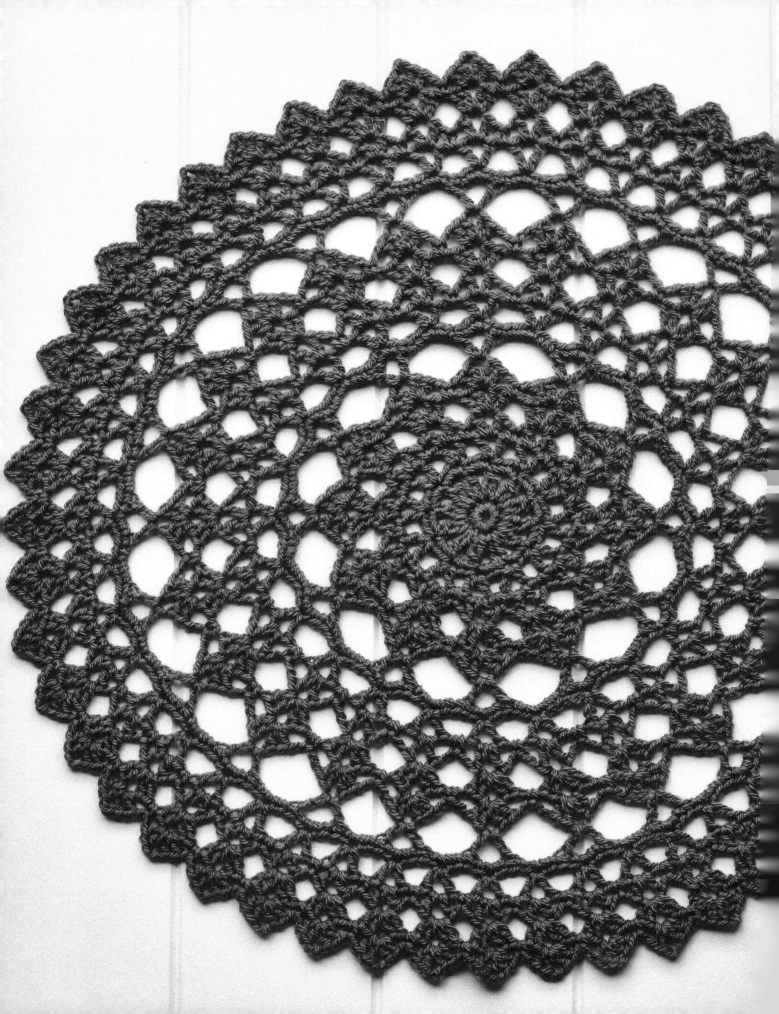

PEACE

MANDALA

noun. freedom of the mind from annoyance, distraction, anxiety, an obsession, etc.

If that ufo is annoying you for all the wrong reasons, get rid of it, be at peace with your decision.

FINISHED SIZE

46cm/18.11in unblocked

MATERIALS

Special DK
One ball

Colour 1 1116 Green

US G-7 / UK 7 / (4.5mm) hook
Yarn Needle
Scissors

NOTES & TIPS

Blocking

If you make this mandala with a stretchy yarn such as an acrylic, it will need blocking.

Do not fasten off after each round unless you are playing around with different colours.

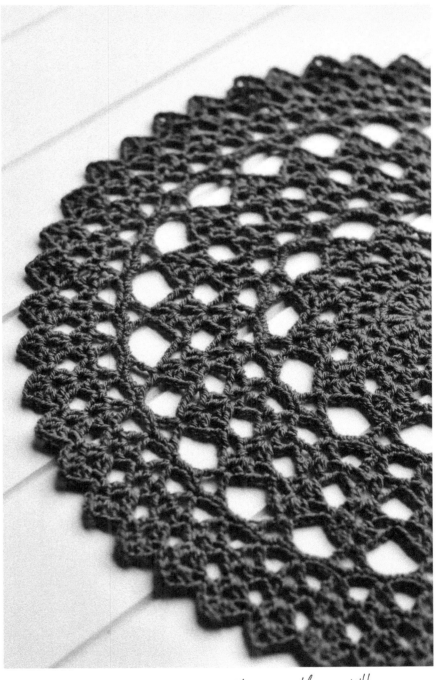

If you cannot find peace within yourself, you will never find it anywhere else.

Marvin Gaye

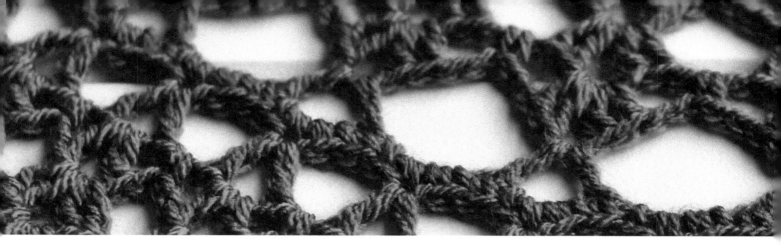

Round 1:

Make a MR, or (ch 6, join to first ch to form ring), ch 1 (doesn't count as st here and throughout), 12 sc in ring, join to first sc made, do not fasten off. *<12 sc>*

Round 2:

Beg dc2cl in same st as join, ch 2, (dc2cl, ch 2) in each st around, join to first cl made, do not fasten off. *<12 dc2cl, 12 ch-2 sp>*

Round 3:

Ch 1, 3 sc in each ch-2 sp around, join to first sc made, do not fasten off. *<36 sc>*

Round 4:

Ch 5 (counts as dc + ch 2 here and through-out), dc in same st as join, ch 1, sk 2 sts, [(dc, ch 2, dc) in next st, ch 1, sk 2 sts] around, join to third ch made, do not fasten off.
<24 dc, 12 ch-2 sp, 12 ch-1 sp>

Round 5:

Sl st to ch-2 sp, (ch 5, dc) in same sp, ch 1, sk st, sc in ch-1 sp, ch 1, sk st, [(dc, ch 2, dc) in next ch-2 sp, ch 1, sk st, sc in next ch-1 sp, ch 1, sk st] around, join to third ch made, do not fasten off.
<24 dc, 12 sc, 12 ch-2 sp, 24 ch-1 sp>

Round 6:

Sl st to ch-2 sp, ch 3, (dc, ch 2, 2 dc) in same sp, ch 2, sk 5 sts, [(2 dc, ch 2, 2 dc) in ch-2 sp, ch 2, sk 5 sts] around, join to third ch made, do not fasten off.
<48 dc, 24 ch-2 sp>

Round 7:

Sl st to ch-2 sp, ch 3 (dc, ch 2, 2 dc) in same sp, ch 1, sk 2 sts, sc in ch-1 sp, ch 1, sk 2 sts, [(2 dc, ch 2, dc) in next ch-2 sp, ch 1, sk 2 sts, sc in ch-2 sp, ch 1, sk 2 sts] around, join to third ch made, do not fasten off. *<48 dc, 24 ch-1 sp, 12 sc, 12 ch-2 sp>*

Round 8:

Sl st to ch-2 sp, ch 6 (counts as dc + ch 3 here and throughout), dc in same sp, ch 5, sk 7 sts, [(dc, ch 3, dc) in ch-2 sp, ch 5, sk 7 sts] around, join to third ch made, do not fasten off. *<24 dc, 12 ch-3 sp, 12 ch-5 sp>*

Round 9:

Ch 1, sc in same st as join, 3 sc in ch-3 sp, sc in st, 5 sc in ch-5 sp, [sc in st, 3 sc in ch-3 sp, sc in st, 5 sc in ch-5 sp] around, join to first sc made, do not fasten off. *<120 sc>*

Round 10:

Sl st to middle sc of first 2-sc grouping, ch 5, dc in same st, ch 2, sk 4 sts, [(dc, ch 2, dc) in next st, ch 2, sk 4 sts] around, join to third ch made, do not fasten off. *<48 dc, 48 ch-2 sp>*

Round 11:

Sl st to ch-2 sp, (ch 5, dc) in same sp, ch 2, sk st, sc in ch-2 sp, ch 2, sk st [(dc, ch 2, dc) in next ch-2 sp, ch 2, sk st, sc in ch-2 sp, ch 2, sk st] around, join to third ch made, do not fasten off. *<48 dc, 24 sc, 72 ch-2 sp>*

Round 12:

Sl st to ch-2 sp, ch 3, (dc, ch 2, 2 dc) in same

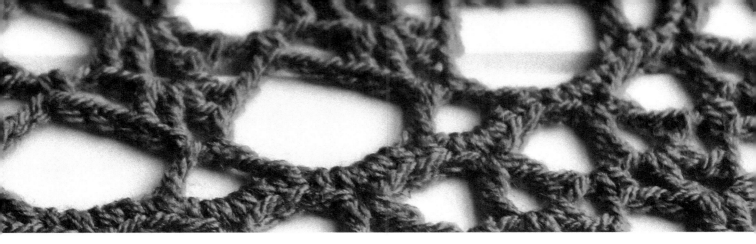

sp, ch 2, sk 7 sts, [(2 dc, ch 2, 2 dc) in next ch-2 sp, ch 2, sk 7 sts] around, join to third ch made, do not fasten off. *<96 dc, 48 ch-2 sp>*

Round 13:

Sl st to ch-2 sp, ch 3, (dc, ch 2, 2 dc) in same sp, ch 2, sk 2 sts, sc in ch-2 sp, ch 2, sk 2 sts, [(2 dc, ch 2, 2 dc) in ch-2 sp, ch 2, sk 2 sts, sc in ch-2 sp, ch 2, sk 2 sts] around, join to third ch made, do not fasten off. *<96 dc, 72 ch-2 sp, 24 sc>*

Round 14:

Sl st to ch-2 sp, ch 6, dc in same sp, ch 3, sk 9 sts, [(dc, ch 3, dc) in next ch-2 sp, ch 3, sk 9 sts] around, join to third ch made, do not fasten off. *<48 dc, 48 ch-3 sp>*

Round 15:

Ch 1, sc in same st as join, 3 sc in ch-3 sp, [sc in st, 3 sc in ch-3 sp] around, join to first sc made, do not fasten off. *<192 sc>*

Round 16:

Sl st to middle sc, ch 5, dc in same st, ch 1, sk 3 sts, [(dc, ch 2, dc) in next st, ch 1, sk 3 sts] around, join to third ch made, do not fasten off. *<96 dc, 48 ch-2 sp, 48 ch-1 sp>*

Round 17:

Sl st to ch-2 sp, (ch 5, dc) in same sp, ch 1, sk st, sc in ch-1 sp, ch 1, sk st, [(dc, ch 2, dc) in next ch-2 sp, ch 1, sk st, sc in ch-1 sp, ch 1, sk st] around, join to third ch made, do not fasten off.

<96 dc, 48 sc, 96 ch-1 sp, 48 ch-2 sp>

Round 18:

Sl st to ch-2 sp, ch 3, (dc, ch 2, 2 dc) in same sp, ch 1, sk 5 sts, [(2 dc, ch 2, 2 dc) in ch-2 sp, ch 1, sk 5 sts] around, join to third ch made, do not fasten off. *<192 dc, 48 ch-2 sp, 48 ch-1 sp>*

Round 19: *This round will ruffle slightly. A nice block or attaching to ring will flatten it.*

Sl st to ch-2 sp, ch 3 (dc, ch 2, 2 dc) in same sp, ch 1, sk 2 sts, sc in ch-1 sp, ch 1, sk 2 sts, [(2 dc, ch 2, 2 dc) in next ch-2 sp, ch 1, sk 2 sts, sc in ch-1 sp, ch 1, sk 2 sts] around, join to third ch made, fasten off. *<192 dc, 48 sc, 48 ch-2 sp, 96 ch-1 sp>*

PEACE

MANDALA

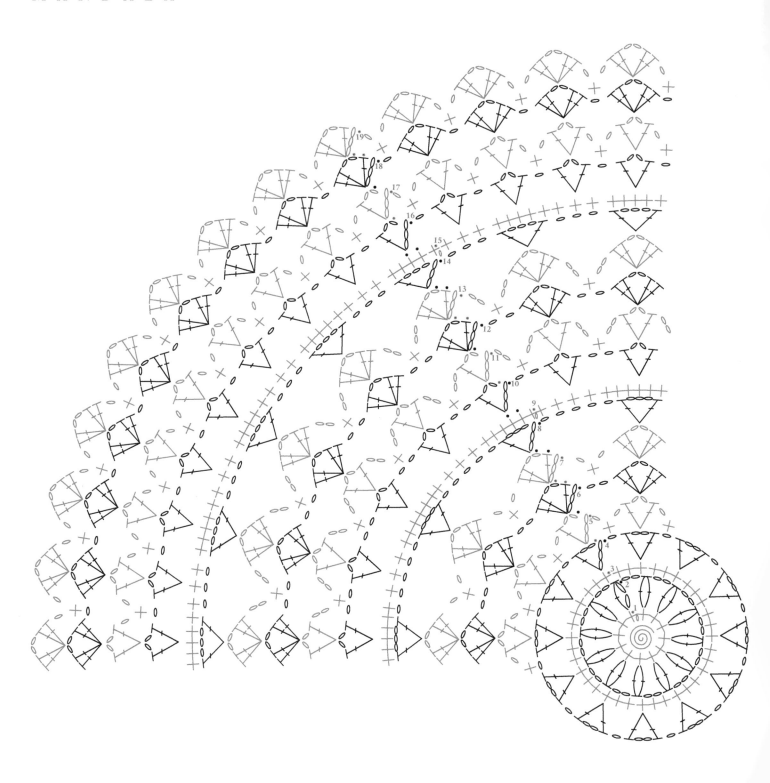

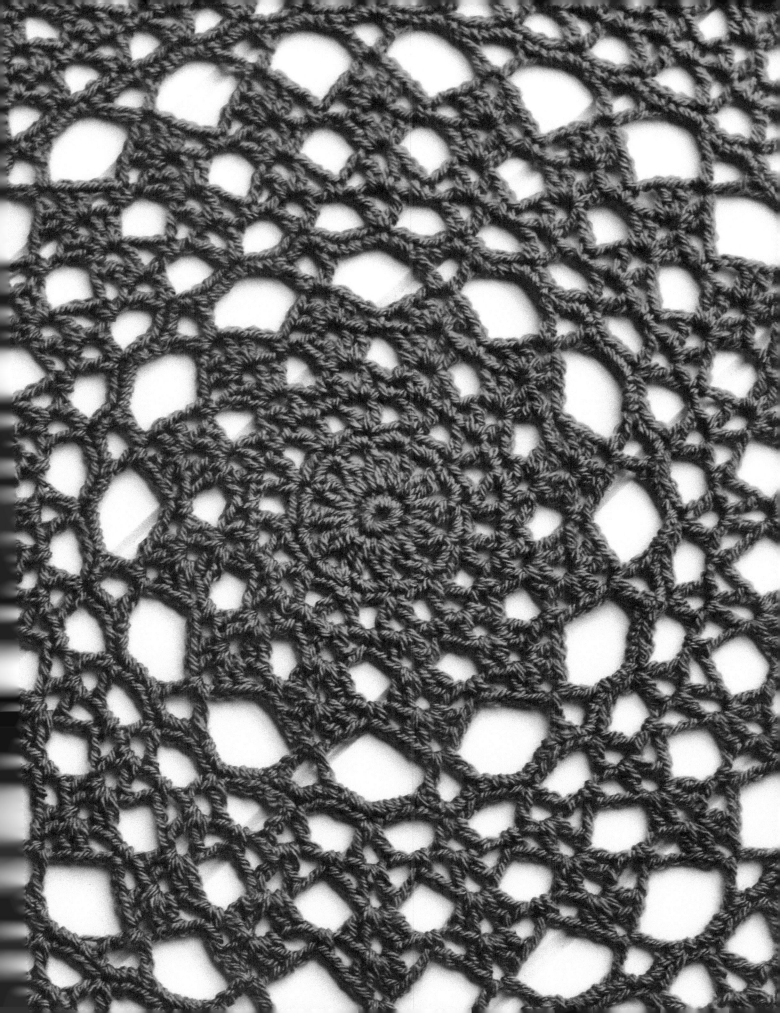

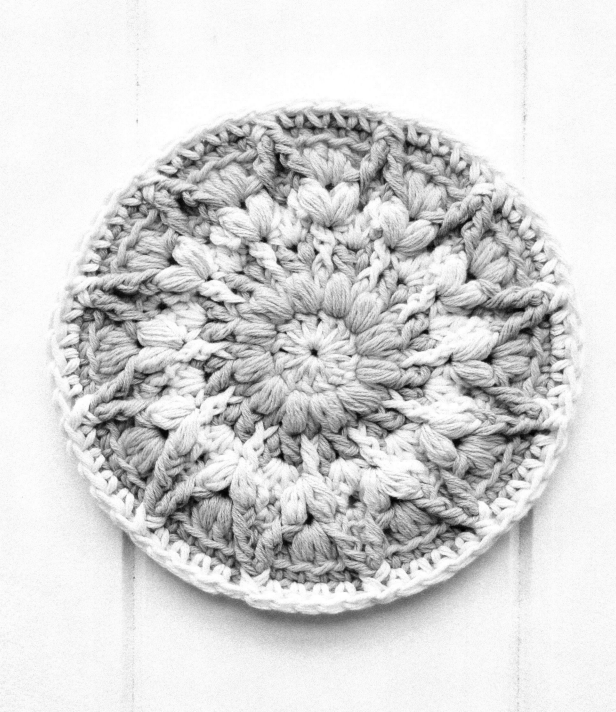

SINCERITY

MANDALA

noun. freedom from deceit, hypocrisy, or duplicity; honesty in intention or in communicating

There is nothing but sincerity when it comes to yourself crocheting, there are no shortcuts. It just is.

FINISHED SIZE

14cm/5.5in unblocked

MATERIALS

Naturals Organic Cotton
One ball of each

Colour 1 7177 Blush
Colour 2 7169 Fondant
Colour 3 7184 Mauve
Colour 4 7172 Peppermint

US G/6 UK 8 (4mm) hook
Yarn Needle
Scissors

NOTES & TIPS

Hearts

Can you spot the little hearts in this pattern? How many can you see?

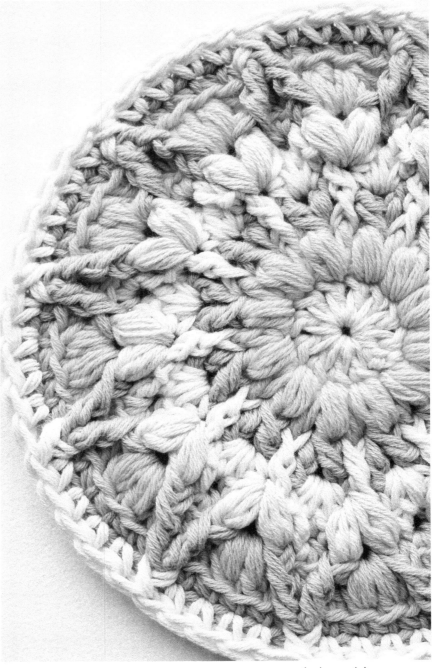

Sincerity means that the appearance and the reality are exactly the same.

Oswald Chambers

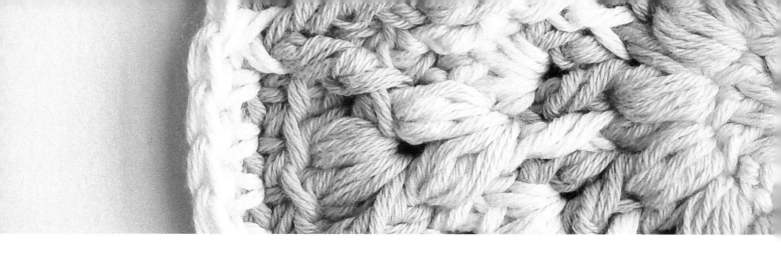

Round 1: C1

Make a MR, or (ch 4, join to first ch to form ring), ch 3 (counts as dc), 11 dc in ring, join to 3rd ch made, fasten off. *<12 dc>*

Round 2: C2

In any st, make a standing (dc, puff 3) in each st, join to first dc made, fasten off.

<12 dc, 12 puff 3>

Round 3: C3

In any dc, make a standing [sc in dc, (fpdc, ch 1, fpdc) around puff] around, join to first sc made, fasten off.

<12 sc, 24 fpdc, 12 ch-1 sp>

Round 4: C4

In any dc from Rnd 2, make a standing [fpdc around dc from Rnd 2, sk st, (hdc, dc, ch 2, dc, hdc) in ch-1 sp from Rnd 3, sk st] around, join to first fpdc made, fasten off. *<12 fpdc, 24 dc, 24 hdc, 12 ch-2 sp>*

Round 5: C1 - *This round may be slightly ruffled but will flatten with following rounds.*

In any ch-2 sp, make a standing [2 sc in ch-2 sp, sk 2 sts, (puff 3, ch 1, puff 3), in fpdc, sk 2 sts] around, join to first sc made, fasten off.

<24 puff 3, 24 sc, 12 ch-1 sp>

Round 6: C2 - *This round will still be slightly ruffled*

In any first sc made after a puff 3, make a standing [2 blo dc in each of next 2 sc sts, sk st, 2 puff 3 in ch-1 sp, sk st] around, join to first blo dc made, fasten off. *<24 puff 3, 48 blo dc>*

Round 7: C3

In any first puff 3 made, make a standing [blo sc in each puff 3 st, blo sc in next dc, fptr2tog around puff 3 from Rnd 5 below sc just made and next puff 3 from Rnd 5, sk 2 sts on Rnd 6, blo sc in next dc] around, join to first blo sc made, fasten off. *<48 blo sc, 12 fptr2tog>*

Round 8: C4

Around any fptr2tog, make a standing [fphdc around fptr2tog, blo hdc in next 4 sts] around, join to first fphdc made, fasten off.

<12 fphdc, 48 blo hdc>

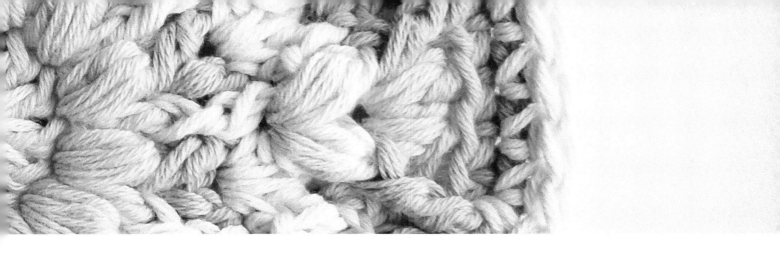

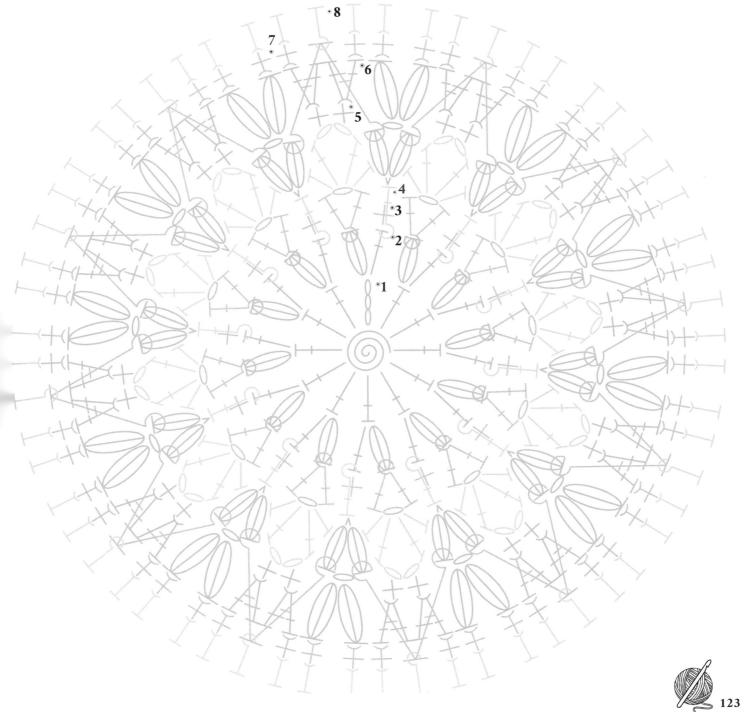

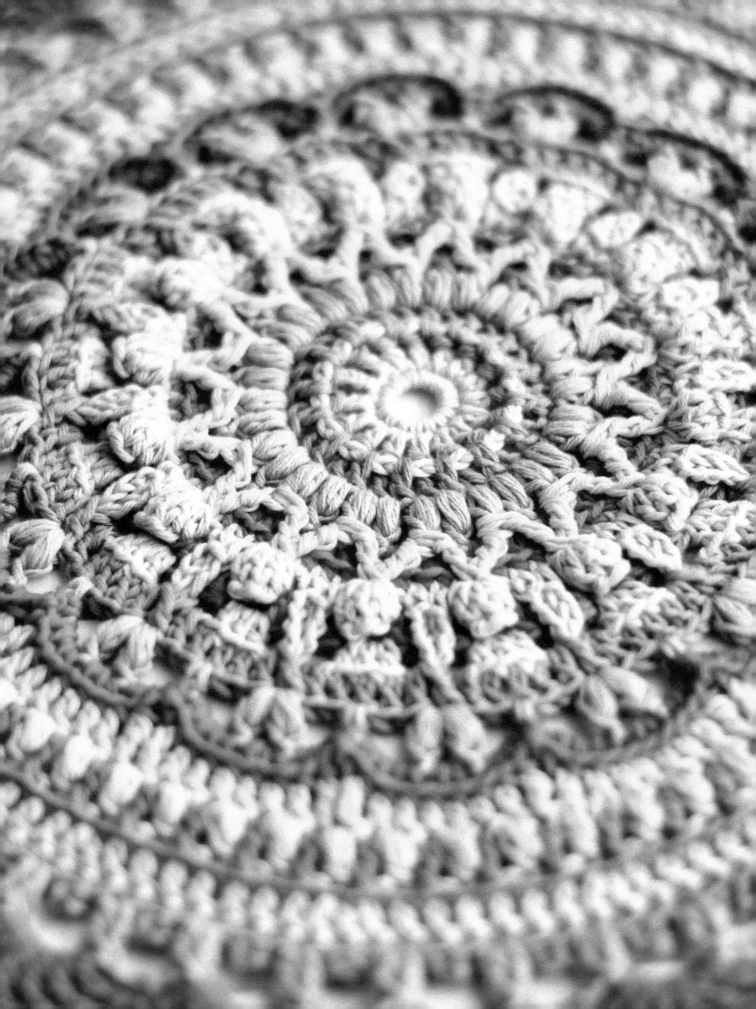

STRENGTH

M A N D A L A

noun. mental power, force, or vigor

If you ever see a crocheter walk out of a craft store with nothing, you have witnessed sheer strength.

FINISHED SIZE

17cm/6.7in unblocked

MATERIALS

Naturals Organic Cotton
One ball of each

Colour 1 7187 Flax
Colour 2 7188 Wood
Colour 3 7189 Rosewood
Colour 4 7186 Plum
Colour 5 7175 Citron
Colour 6 7193 Artichoke
Colour 7 7200 Blue Dusk

US G/6 UK 8 (4mm) hook
Yarn Needle
Scissors
Stitch Marker

NOTES & TIPS

Round 10
Make sure you make the fp st around
both ch-5 sts together.

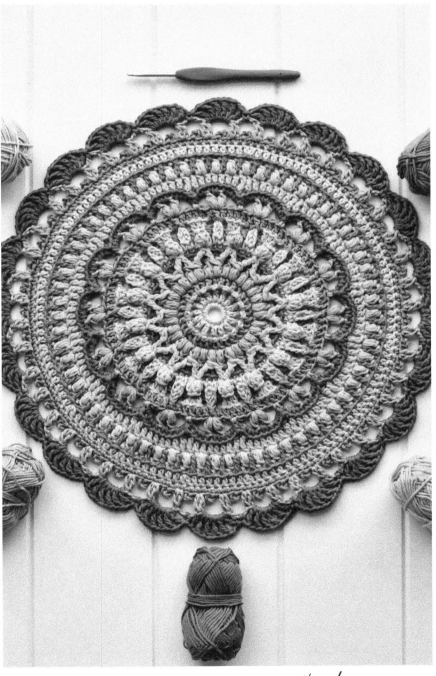

*A calm mind brings inner strength and
self-confidence*

Dalai Lama

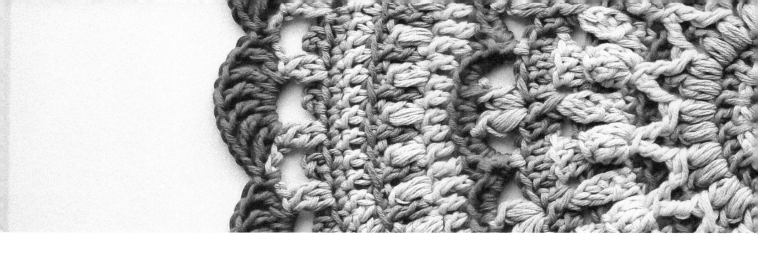

Round 1: C1

Make a MR, or (ch 8, join to first ch to form ring), ch 1 (doesn't count as st), 16 sc in ring, do not fasten off. *<16 sc>*

Round 2: C1

Ch 4 (counts as dc + ch 1), (dc, ch 1) in each st around, join to third ch made, fasten off. *<16 dc, 16 ch-1 sp>*

Round 3: C2

In any ch-1 sp, make a standing [dc in ch-1 sp, bpdc around st] around, join to first dc made, fasten off. *<16 dc, 16 bpdc>*

Round 4: C3

In any st, make a standing (puff 3, ch 1) in each st around, join to first puff made, fasten off. *<32 puff 3, 32 ch-1 sp>*

Round 5: C4

In any ch-1 sp, make a standing [2 dc in ch-1 sp, sk puff 3] around, join to first dc made, fasten off. *<64 dc>*

Round 6: C5

In first dc made in prev rnd, make blo sc in st, blo sc in next 3 sts, [fptr2tog around puff before puff below, skip below puff and finish fptr2tog around next puff, blo sc in next 4 sts] around, join to first blo sc made, fasten off. Place marker in first fptr2tog made. *<16 fptr2tog, 64 blo sc>*

Round 7: C6

In st marker, make [pop in fptr2tog, ch 1, blo sc in next 4 sts, ch 1] around, join to first pop made, fasten off. Place st marker in first sc after pop. *<64 blo sc, 16 pop, 32 ch-1 sp>*

Round 8: C7

In st marker, dc dec over next 2 sts, ch 1, dc dec over next 2 sts, ch 2, sk pop, [dc dec over next 2 sts, ch 1, dc dec over next 2 sts, ch 2, sk pop] around, join to first dc dec made, fasten off. *<32 dc dec, 16 ch-1 sp, 16 ch-2 sp>*

Round 9: C1

[3 dc in ch-2 sp, ch 5, sk dc dec, flo sc in middle 2 sc from Rnd 6, ch 5, sk dc dec] around, join to first dc made, fasten off. Place st marker in first dc made. *<32 flo sc, 48 dc, 32 ch-5 sp>*

Round 10: C2

In st marker, make [blo dc in each of next 3 dc, dc in ch-sp, fpdc around both ch-5 loops together, dc in ch-sp] around, join to first blo dc made, fasten off. Place st marker in first fpdc made. *<32 dc, 48 blo dc, 16 fpdc>*

Round 11: C3

In st marker, make [(puff 3, ch 1, puff 3) in fpdc, ch 3, sk 2 sts, sc in next st, ch 3, sk 2 sts] around, join to first puff made, fasten off. Place st marker in last sc made. *<32 puff 3, 32 sc, 16 ch-1 sp, 32 ch-3 sp>*

Round 12: C4 - *This round may be slightly ruffled but will flatten out with following rounds*

In st marker, make [fpsc around sc, 3 hdc in ch-3 sp, hdc in st, 2 hdc in ch-1 sp, hdc in st,

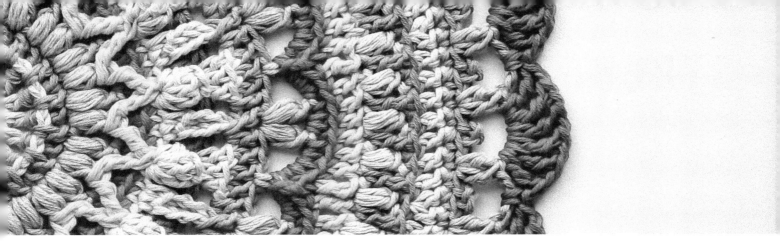

3 hdc in ch-3 sp] around, join to first fpsc made, fasten off. Place st marker in 2nd hdc made. *<160 hdc, 16 fpsc>*

Round 13: C5

In st marker, make a standing [blo tr, blo dc in each of next 6 sts, blo tr in next st, sk 3 sts] around, join to first blo tr made, fasten off. Place st marker in first blo tr made. *<32 blo tr, 96 blo dc>*

Round 14: C7

In st marker, make a standing [puff 3, ch 2, sk st] around, join to first puff 3 made, fasten off. Place st marker in first puff made. *<64 puff 3, 64 ch-2 sp>*

Round 15: C1

In st marker, make a standing [sc in puff 3, tr in unworked st from Rnd 13] around, join to first sc, fasten off. Place st marker in first sc made. *<64 tr, 64 sc>*

Round 16: C2 – *This round is worked in back and third loops only*

In st marker, make a standing [2 blo dc in st, blo dc in each of next 7 sts] around, join to first blo dc made, fasten off. Place st marker in first dc made. *<144 blo dc>*

Round 17: C3

In st marker, make a sc, sc in next st, picot 3, [sc in each of next 3 sts, picot 3] around, on final repeat, make sc in last st, join to first sc made, fasten off. Place st marker in first sc made. *<144 sc, 48 picot 3>*

Round 18: C4

In st marker, make a standing [dc2cl, ch 3, sk st, sk picot, sk st] around, join to first dc2cl made, fasten off. Place st marker in first ch-3 sp made. *<48 dc2cl, 48 ch-3 sp>*

Round 19: C5

In st marker sp, make a [(tr, ch 1) 5 times in ch-3 sp, tr in same sp, sk st, sc in next ch-3 sp, sk st] around, join to first tr made, fasten off. *<144 tr, 120 ch-1 sp, 24 sc>*

STRENGTH

MANDALA

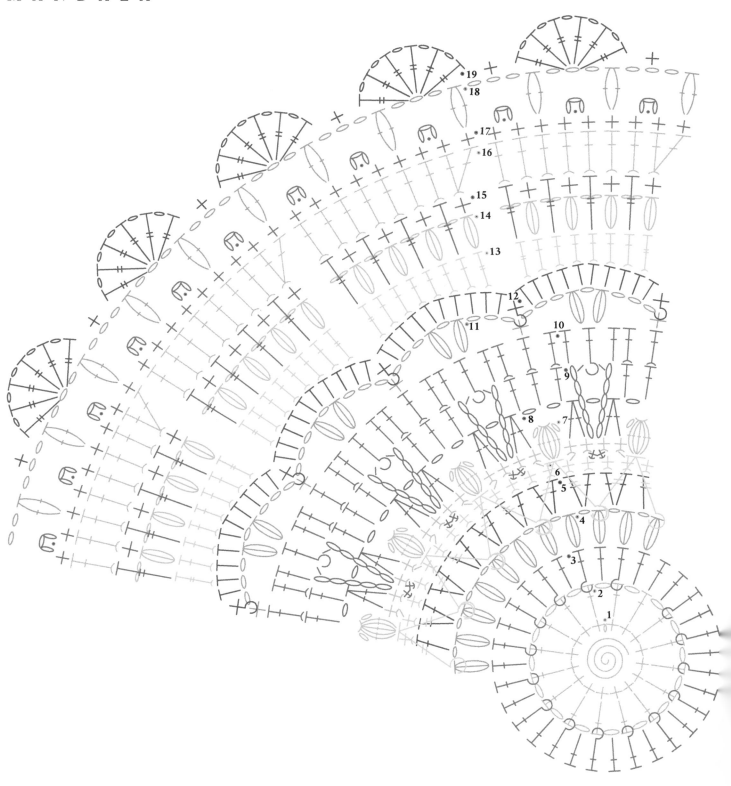

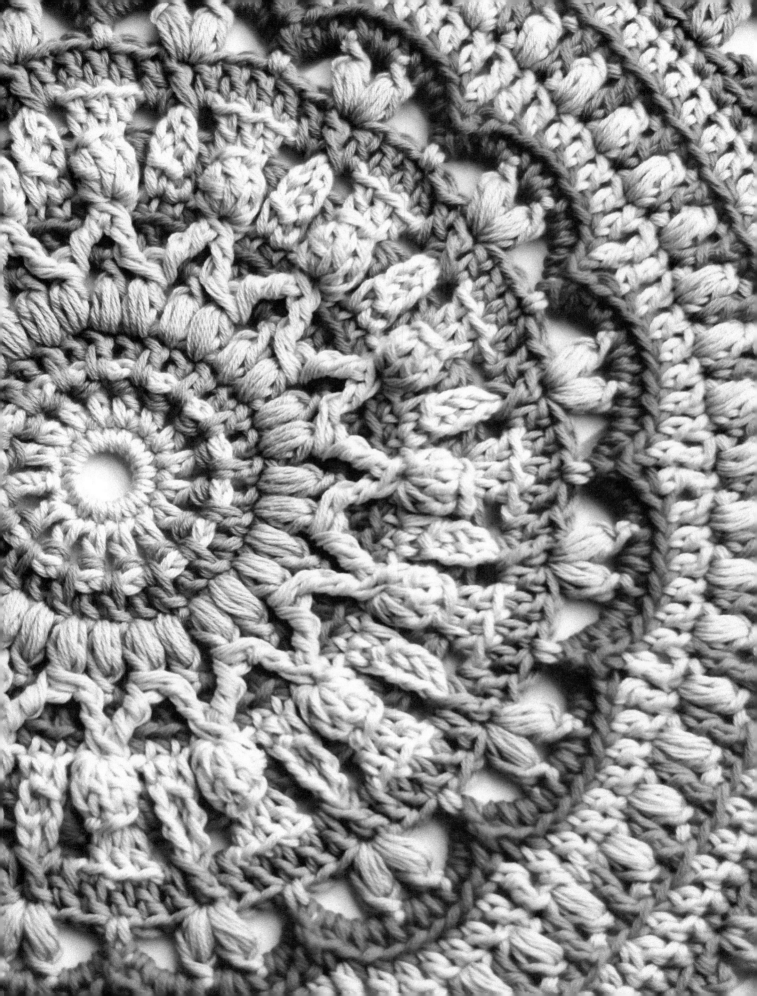

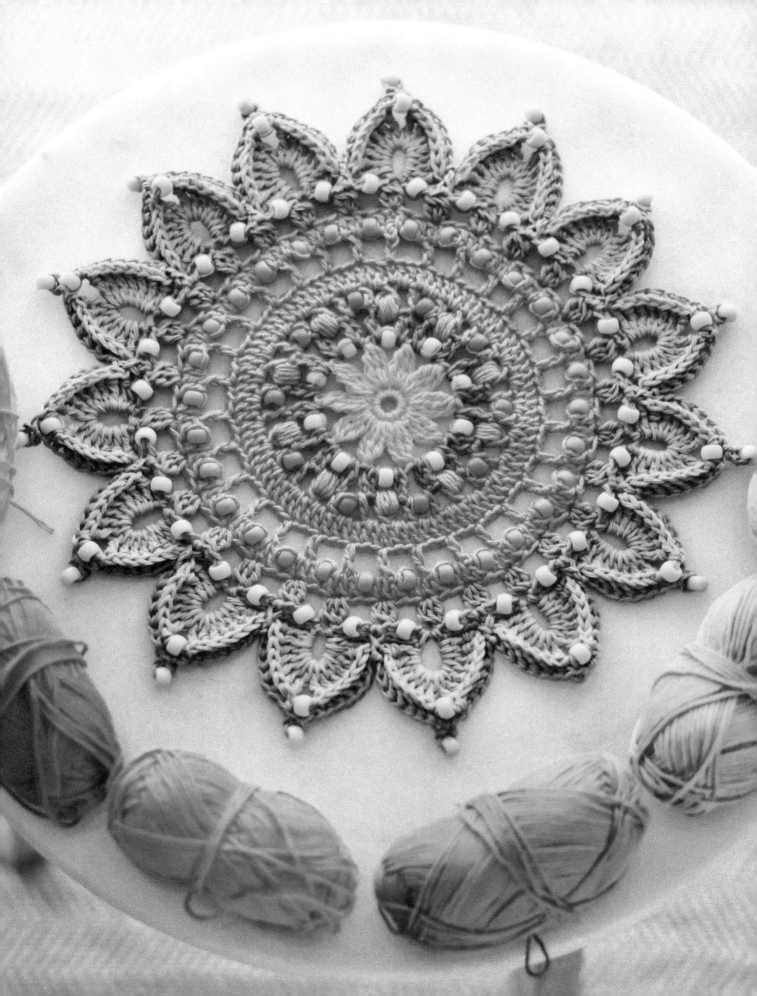

TRUSTWORTHY

M A N D A L A

adjective. deserving of trust or confidence; dependable; reliable

Trustworthy is the fellow crocheter who will stop talking to you while you are counting.

FINISHED SIZE

31cm/12.2in unblocked

MATERIALS

Naturals Organic Cotton
One ball of each

Colour 1 7179 Flamingo
Colour 2 7185 Amethyst
Colour 3 7198 Azure
Colour 4 7192 Sea Green
Colour 5 7191 Jade
Colour 6 7171 Leaf

US G/6 UK 8 (4mm) hook
Yarn Needle
Scissors
Stitch Marker
Beads see below

NOTES & TIPS

3mm Beads required

Round 2: 10 Beads
Round 3: 10 Beads
Round 6: 30 Beads
Round 8: 30 Beads
Round 10: 15 Beads
Round 11: 15 Beads

Feel free to complement (match) or contrast (opposite) the colours in your rounds with the beads.

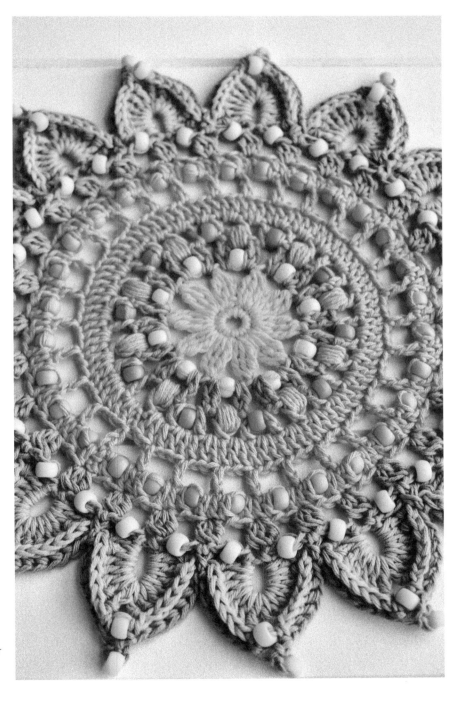

He who does not trust enough will not be trusted.

Lao Tzu

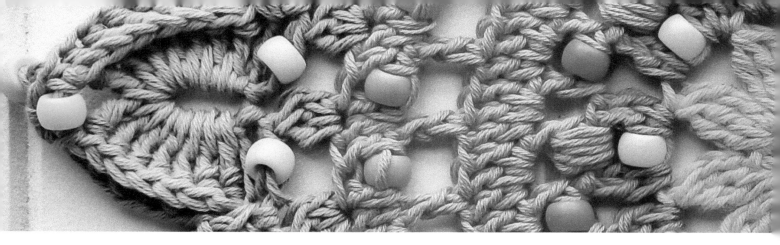

Round 1: C1

Make a MR, or (ch 5, join to first ch to form ring), ch 1 (doesn't count as st), 10 sc in ring, join to first sc made, do not fasten off. *<10 sc>*

Round 2: C1

Make a beg tr3cl, ch 1, IB, ch 1, (tr3cl, ch 1, IB, ch 1) in each st around, join to first cl made, fasten off. *<10 tr3cl, 20 ch-1 sp, 10 beads>*

Round 3: C2

In ch-1 sp before bead, make a standing [2 dc in ch-1 sp, ch 1, sk bead, 2 dc in ch-1 sp after bead, ch 1, IB, sk cl, ch 1] around, join to first dc made, fasten off. *<40 dc, 30 ch-1 sp, 10 beads>*

Round 4: C3

In ch-1 sp between dc pairs (not one with a bead), make a standing [puff 5 in ch-1 sp above bead from Rnd 2, ch 1, sk 2 sts, dc in next ch-1 sp, ch 1, skip bead, dc in next ch-1 sp, ch 1, sk 2 sts] around, join to first puff 5 made, do not fasten off. *<10 puff 5, 20 dc, 30 ch-1 sp>*

Round 5: C3 – This round may be slightly ruffled

Ch 3 (counts as dc here and throughout), 2 dc in ch-1 sp, [dc in next st, 2 dc in ch-1 sp] around, join to 3rd ch made, do not fasten off. *<90 dc>*

Round 6: C3

Ch 5 (counts as tr + ch 1), IB, ch 1, sk 2 sts, [tr in next st, ch 1, IB, ch 1, sk 2 sts] around, join to 4th ch made, do not fasten off. *<30 beads, 60 ch-1 sp, 30 tr>*

Round 7: C3 – This may still be slightly ruffled

Ch 3, dc in ch-1 sp, sk bead, dc in ch-1 sp, [dc in st, dc in ch-1 sp, sk bead, dc in ch-1 sp] around, join to 3rd ch made, fasten off. *<90 dc>*

Round 8: C4

In a dc in a tr from Rnd 6, make a standing [dc3cl in middle dc, ch 1, IB, ch 1, sk 2 sts] around, join to first dc3cl made, do not fasten off. *<30 dc3cl, 30 beads, 60 ch-1 sp>*

Round 9: C4

Ch 7, sl st in same st, ch 4, sk ch sts and bead, sc in next cl, ch 4, sk ch sts and bead, [sl st, ch 7, sl st) in cl, ch 4, sk ch sts and bead, sc in next cl, ch 4, sk ch sts and bead] around, join to first cl, fasten off. *<15 ch-7, 30 ch-4 sp, 15 sc>*

Round 10: C5

In any ch-7 loop, make a standing [(7 tr, ch 1, IB, ch 1, 7 tr, in ch-7 sp, sl st in sc] around, join to first tr made, fasten off. *<210 tr, 15 beads, 30 ch-1 sp, 15 sc, 30 sl st>*

Round 11: C6

Make a standing [fpsc around sc from Rnd 9, bphdc next 7 tr, hdc in ch-1 sp, ch 2, IB, ch 2, sl st in first ch st before bead, sk IB, hdc in ch-1 sp, bphdc around next 7 tr] around, join to first fpsc made, fasten off. *<15 fpsc, 255 bphdc, 30 hdc, 15 beads, 60 ch-2 sp>*

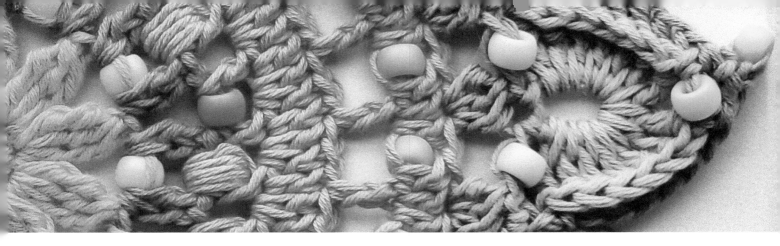

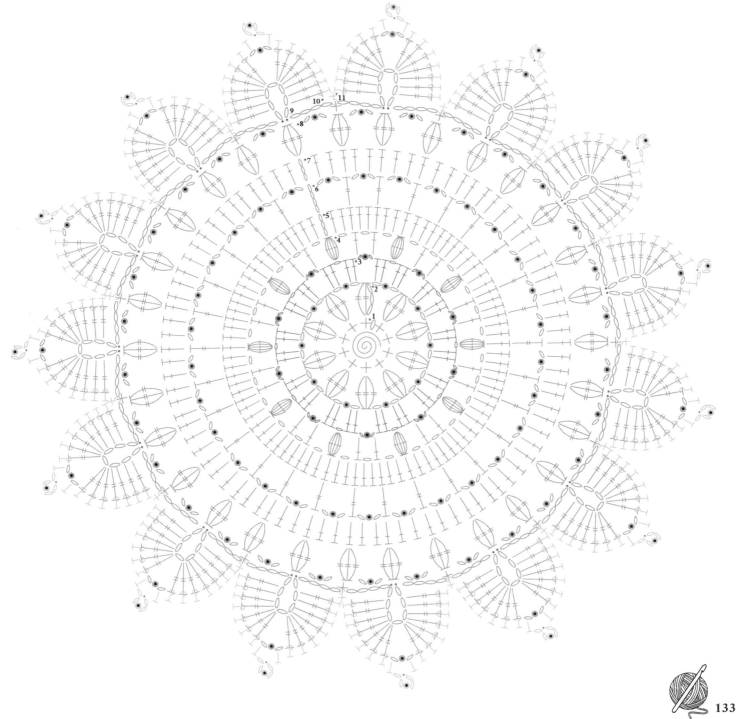

GLOSSARY

Abbreviations

MR	magic ring	
st/s	stitch/es	
sp/s	space/s	
prev	previous	
rnd/s	round/s	
yo	yarn over	Wrap yarn from back to front around hook.
	3rd loop	The loop behind the v (is seen by looking at both back and front loops from above)
	standing stitch	Make indicated stitch with either slip knot on hook or without. Finish round with invisible join if using no slip knot.
	invisible join	Complete round, cut yarn, pull tail through. Thread tail onto yarn needle, insert needle from front to back under both top loops of the second stitch made, insert needle into the top of the stitch where the tail came from and pull out of the back of the stitch. Weave in ends.
IB	insert bead	Drop loop from working hook, pick up smaller hook, insert bead onto hook, pick up dropped loop, and pull through bead, drop loop off small hook, swap back to working hook.

Stitches & Techniques

ch	chain	
sl st	slip stitch	
sc	single crochet	Insert hook into stitch or space indicated, yo and draw up a loop, yo and pull through both loops on hook.
fpsc	front post single crochet	Insert hook from front to back to front around post of stitch indicated, yo and draw up a loop, yo and pull through both loops on hook.
blo	back loop only	Make stitch into the back and third loop of stitch indicated.
sc dec	single crochet decrease	Insert hook in stitch or space indicated, yo and draw up a loop, insert hook into next stitch or space indicated, yo and draw up a loop, yo and pull through all three loops on hook.
hdc	half double crochet	Yo once, insert hook into stitch or space indicated, yo and draw up a loop, yo and pull through all three loops on hook.
bphdc	back post half double crochet	Yo once, insert hook from back to front to back around stitch indicated, yo and draw up a loop, yo and pull through all three loops on hook.
fphdc	front post half double crochet	Yo once, insert hook from front to back to front around stitch indicated, yo and draw up a loop, yo and pull through all three loops on hook.
dc	double crochet	Yo once, insert hook into stitch indicated, yo and draw up a loop, (yo and pull through two loops) two times.

GLOSSARY

fpdc	front post double crochet	Yo once, insert hook from front to back to front around stitch indicated, yo and draw up a loop, (yo and pull through two loops) two times.
dc dec	double crochet decrease	Yo, insert hook into stitch or space indicated, yo and pull up a loop, yo and pull through two loops, yo and insert hook into NEXT stitch or space indicated, yo and pull up a loop, yo and pull through two loops, yo and pull through three loops on hook.
dc3dec	double crochet 3 decrease	Yo, insert hook into stitch or space indicated, pull up a loop, yo and pull through two loops, [yo, insert hook into next stitch or space indicated, pull up a loop, yo and pull through two loops] two times, yo and pull through four loops on hook.
beg dc2cl	beginning double crochet 2 cluster	Ch 2 (counts as first part of cluster), yo once, insert hook into stitch or space indicated, yo and draw up a loop, yo and pull through two loops, yo and pull through both loops on hook.
beg dc3cl	beginning double crochet 3 cluster	Ch 2 (counts as part of cluster), *yo, insert hook into stitch or space indicated, yo and draw up a loop, yo and pull through two loops*, leaving two loops on hook, repeat from * to *, leaving three loops on hook, yo and pull through all three loops on hook.
dc2cl	double crochet 2 cluster	(Yo once, insert hook into stitch or space indicated, yo and draw up a loop, yo and pull through two loops) twice, yo and pull through all three loops on hook.
dc3cl	double crochet 3 cluster	[Yo, insert hook into stitch or space indicated, yo and draw up a loop, yo and pull through two loops] three times, leaving three loops on hook, yo and pull through all loops on hook.
tr	treble crochet	Yo twice, insert hook into stitch or space indicated, yo and draw up a loop, (yo and pull through two loops) three times.
fptr	front post treble crochet	Yo twice, insert hook from front to back to front around post of stitch indicated, yo and draw up a loop, (yo and pull through two loops) three times.
beg tr2cl	beginning treble 2 cluster	Ch 3 (counts as first part of treble cluster), yo twice, insert hook in stitch or space indicated, yo and draw up a loop, (yo and pull through two loops) twice, leaving two loops on hook, yo and pull through both loops on hook.
tr2cl	treble 2 cluster	*Yo twice, insert hook in stitch or space indicated, yo and draw up a loop (yo and pull through two loops) twice*, leaving two loops on hook. Repeat from * to * once and pull through all three loops on hook.
beg tr3cl	beginning treble 3 cluster	Ch 3 (counts as the first part of treble cluster), *yo twice, insert hook in stitch or space indicated, yo and draw up a loop, (yo and pull through two loops) two times*, leaving two loops on hook, repeat from * to * once, then yo and pull through all three loops on hook.

GLOSSARY

tr3cl	treble 3 cluster	*Yo twice, insert hook in stitch or space indicated, yo and draw up a loop (yo and pull through two loops) two times*, leaving two loops on hook. Repeat from * to * two times then yo and pull through all four loops on hook.
beg tr4cl	beginning treble 4 cluster	Ch 3 (counts as first part), [Yo two times, insert hook into stitch or space indicated, yo and pull up a loop, (yo and pull through two loops) two times] three times, yo and pull through all four loops on hook.
tr4cl	treble 4 cluster	[Yo two times, insert hook into stitch or space indicated, yo and pull up a loop, (yo and pull through two loops) two times] four times, yo and pull through all five loops on hook.
tr6cl	treble 6 cluster	With loop on hook, *yo twice, insert hook into stitch or space indicated, yo and pull up a loop, (yo and pull through two loops) twice*, repeat from * to * two more times on one side of popcorn, repeat from * to * 3 times on other side of popcorn, yo, pull through all seven loops on hook.
fptr2tog	front post treble 2 together	Yo twice, insert hook from front to back to front around stitch indicated, pull up a loop, (yo and pull through two loops) two times, yo twice and insert hook around next stitch indicated, pull up a loop, (yo and pull through two loops) two times, yo and pull through all three loops on hook.
crossover tr		Work tr stitch in stitch indicated, ch 1, work next tr in stitch prev to first tr made, sk unworked st.
pop	popcorn	Work 5 dc into stitch or space indicated, drop loop from hook, insert into first dc made, pick up dropped loop and pull through first st.
puff 3	puff 3	(Yo, insert hook into stitch or space indicated and pull up a loop) three times, yo and pull through six loops, yo and pull through last two loops on hook.
puff 5	puff 5	(Yo, insert hook into stitch or space indicated and pull up a loop) five times, yo and pull through 10 loops, yo and pull through last two loops on hook.
picot 3		Ch 3, slip stitch in front loop and last leg of stitch prior to ch-3 stitches.
picot 5		Ch 5, slip stitch in front loop and last leg of stitch prior to ch-5 stitches.
v st		Make (dc, ch 1, dc) in stitch or space indicated.
fpdtr	front post double treble crochet	Yo three times, insert hook from front to back to front around indicated stitch, pull up a loop, (yo and pull through two loops) four times.
dtr2cl	double treble crochet 2 cluster	[Yo three times, insert hook into stitch or space indicated, yo and draw up a loop, (yo and pull through two loops) three times] two times, leaving two loops on hook, yo and pull through all three loops on hook.

GLOSSARY

dtr2cl	double treble crochet 2 cluster	[Yo three times, insert hook into stitch or space indicated, yo and draw up a loop, (yo and pull through two loops) three times] two times, leaving two loops on hook, yo and pull through all three loops on hook.
fphdc2tog	front post half double crochet 2 together	Yo, insert hook around stitch indicated from front to back to front, yo and pull up a loop, yo and insert hook around next stitch indicated from front to back to front, yo and pull up a loop, yo and pull through five loops on hook.
x st	x st	With slip knot on hook or working loop on hook, yo twice, insert hook into stitch or space indicated, yo and pull up a loop, yo and pull through two loops, sk st, yo and insert hook into next stitch or space indicated, yo and pull up a loop, (yo and pull through two loops) three times, ch 2, yo and insert hook into 2 middle front loops of stitch just made, yo and pull up a loop, (yo and pull through two loops) two times.

CROCHET HOOK SIZES

METRIC	US	UK/CANADA
2.00mm	-	14
2.25mm	B-1	13
2.50mm	-	12
2.75mm	C-2	-
3.00mm	-	11
3.125mm	D	-
3.25mm	D-3	10
3.50mm	E-4	9
3.75mm	F-5	-
4.00mm	G-6	8
4.25mm	G	-
4.50mm	7	7
5.00mm	H-8	6
5.25mm	I	-
5.50mm	I-9	5
6.00mm	J-10	4
6.50mm	K	3
7.00mm	-	2
8.00mm	L-11	0
9.00mm	M/N-13	00
10.00mm	N/P-15	000

SYMBOLS USED

[ ]　　Work instructions within brackets as many times as directed

( )　　Work instructions within parentheses in same stitch or space indicated

* *　　Repeat the instructions between asterisks as many times as directed

< >　　These brackets consist of the stitch count per round.

NOTES

Throughout this book, I use standing stitches to start each round when a new colour is used. This replaces joining with a slip stitch and chaining the appropriate length required. To finish these rounds, I use and recommend invisible joins.

Scan the QR Code to watch a video on how to make Standing Stitches. →

Scan the QR Code to watch a video on how to make Invisible Joins. →

If you are unable to scan the codes, you can find these videos on my YouTube Channel by searching for 'The Loopy Stitch'.

I try to write my patterns so that all skill levels can understand them. That in mind, some may find them trickier, depending on your crochet and pattern reading experience. I would recommend having a go, breaking it down to more smaller manageable pieces and going from there. I do have a Facebook Group where you can also share your pieces made by my patterns, ask for help and connect with other like-minded crocheters. If you search 'The Loopy Stitch CAL (Crochet-Along) Group', you will need to request to join and complete the answers accordingly.

I have also included quotes, definitions and have tried to link each pattern name directly with crochet, just for some fun and a personal touch. These quotes were found on Google and the definitions were found on Dictionary.com.

I'd love to know if you have a favourite saying, quote or mandala. Feel free to send me finished photos, questions, or wip photos to theloopystitches@gmail.com.

As this book has been self-published by myself, a human being, there may be typographical errors. If you do come across anything please let me know by reaching out to the email address above.

HOW TO INSERT BEADS

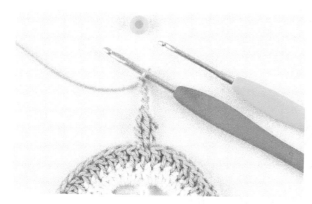

Finish last step in pattern before inserting bead, e.g. last ch st then drop hook from loop.

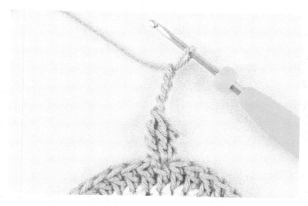

With smaller hook, pick up bead with hook, then pick up dropped loop.

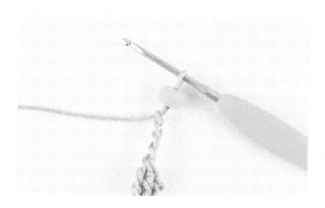

Pull loop through bead.

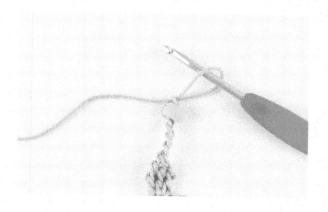

Change back to working hook, make pattern as instructed.

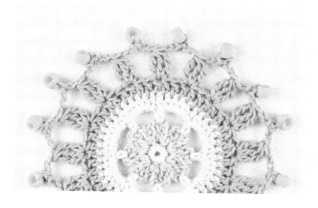

Ta-daa! Pretty beads. It may take a few goes to find what feels natural to you, but you will get it and you will have added something else to your crochet library.

STITCH KEY

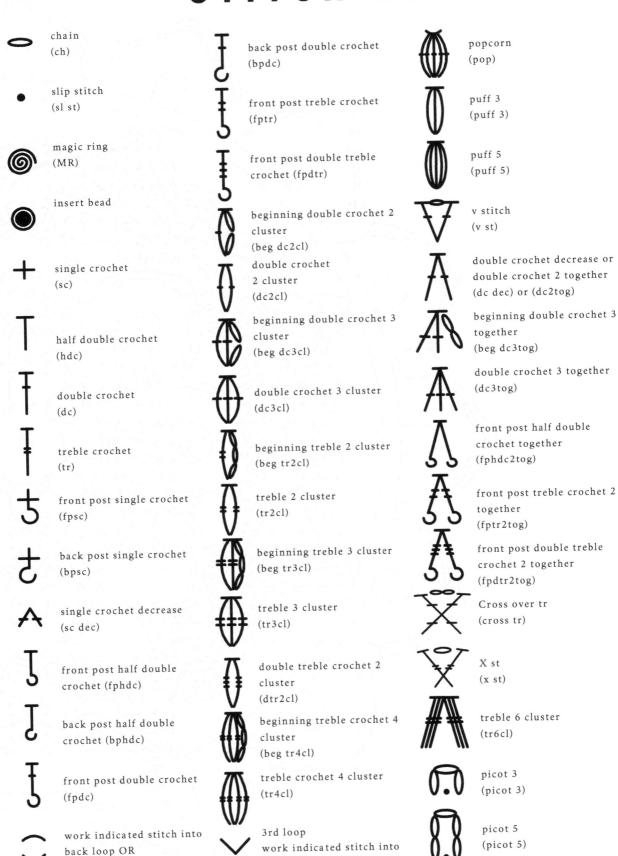

chain
(ch)

slip stitch
(sl st)

magic ring
(MR)

insert bead

single crochet
(sc)

half double crochet
(hdc)

double crochet
(dc)

treble crochet
(tr)

front post single crochet
(fpsc)

back post single crochet
(bpsc)

single crochet decrease
(sc dec)

front post half double
crochet (fphdc)

back post half double
crochet (bphdc)

front post double crochet
(fpdc)

work indicated stitch into
back loop OR
front loop

back post double crochet
(bpdc)

front post treble crochet
(fptr)

front post double treble
crochet (fpdtr)

beginning double crochet 2
cluster
(beg dc2cl)

double crochet
2 cluster
(dc2cl)

beginning double crochet 3
cluster
(beg dc3cl)

double crochet 3 cluster
(dc3cl)

beginning treble 2 cluster
(beg tr2cl)

treble 2 cluster
(tr2cl)

beginning treble 3 cluster
(beg tr3cl)

treble 3 cluster
(tr3cl)

double treble crochet 2
cluster
(dtr2cl)

beginning treble crochet 4
cluster
(beg tr4cl)

treble crochet 4 cluster
(tr4cl)

3rd loop
work indicated stitch into
3rd loop

popcorn
(pop)

puff 3
(puff 3)

puff 5
(puff 5)

v stitch
(v st)

double crochet decrease or
double crochet 2 together
(dc dec) or (dc2tog)

beginning double crochet 3
together
(beg dc3tog)

double crochet 3 together
(dc3tog)

front post half double
crochet together
(fphdc2tog)

front post treble crochet 2
together
(fptr2tog)

front post double treble
crochet 2 together
(fpdtr2tog)

Cross over tr
(cross tr)

X st
(x st)

treble 6 cluster
(tr6cl)

picot 3
(picot 3)

picot 5
(picot 5)

YARN USED

This book is made up exclusively of four types of Stylecraft Yarns: Stylecraft Naturals Organic Cotton; Stylecraft Naturals Bamboo and Cotton; Stylecraft Special Double Knit (DK); Stylecraft Special Aran. The majority of the patterns are made with Organic Cotton, purely as a personal preference because I love how the natural fibres glide effortlessly over the hook.

I have included the overall yarn required for each pattern. Most designs allow for one ball of each colour with ample yarn left over after completion.

Feel free to play around with colours and colour placement, and also the yarn. Please note that I have given approximate sizes using the hooks and yarn mentioned for each pattern.

You will notice I do not mention a gauge when it comes to mandalas. This is due to you, the crocheter maybe wanting to use any yarn, your tension and hook size etc. There are quite a few variables when it comes to gauges and mandalas. But I believe, if you have your yarn that you love and you know the hook that works best with that yarn and want to use that, then go ahead, stick with what you know.

I purchase my Stylecraft Yarn online and usually select the expensive shipping option as regular shipping can take a while to arrive to the land down under, and I'm impatient and want my yarn in my hands and on my hook yesterday. I'm sure a lot of you would be the same.

If you can't access the yarn you need or want to try, I recommend yarnsub.com. This website helps find close matches to the yarn you are searching for. It's a great tool to add to your crochet library. Genius really.

HOOKS

As mentioned above, you will know what hook size works with the yarn you use most often.
Feel free to play around though. If you have never used these types of yarn and notice cupping, go up a hook size. The same as if you're noticing larger than normal gaps and space, try going down a size.

When you make the mandalas that contain beads, you will need a smaller size for inserting the beads. This will depend on the hook and yarn you're using to make the project but mainly the beads. See the previous page for how to insert beads using the method I use in this book. Game changer! No more threading beads on before hand.

I work with five different hook sizes throught this book: 2.5mm; 3.5mm; 4.00mm; 4.50mm and 5.00mm. Hook sizes are stated on each pattern as a guide.

NOTES

MAKING MANDALAS

NOTES

MAKING MANDALAS

NOTES

MAKING MANDALAS

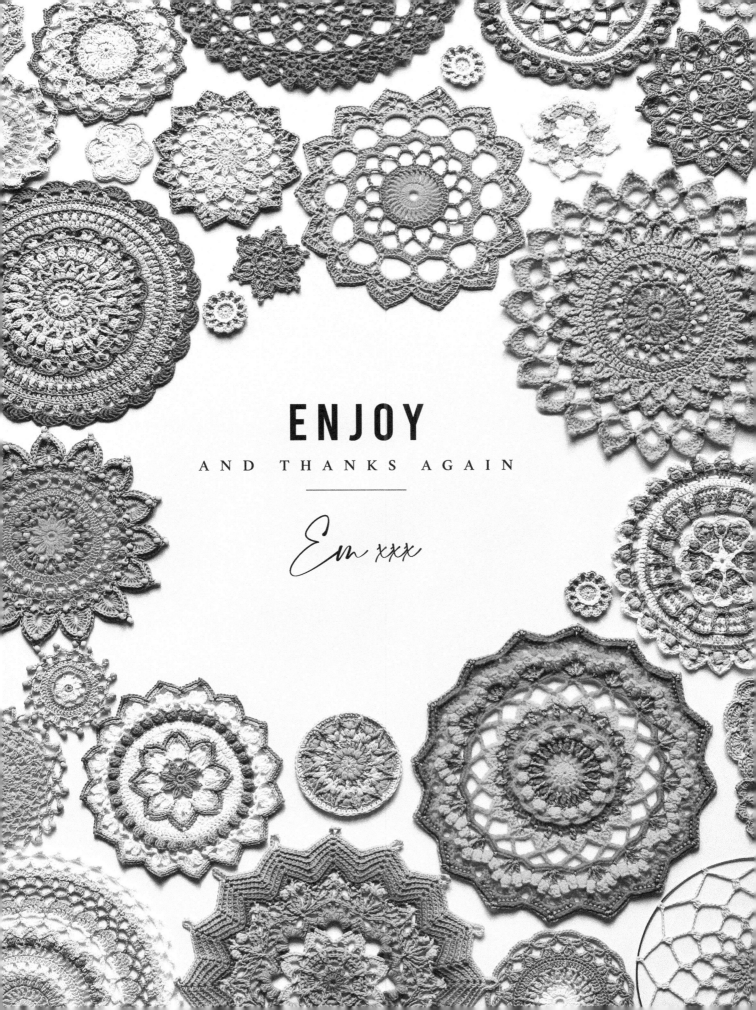

ENJOY

AND THANKS AGAIN

———

Em xxx